Crossings 28

Italians in America

Italians in America

Amerigo Ruggiero

Edited and translated by
Mark Pietralunga

BORDIGHERA PRESS

Published by
BORDIGHERA PRESS
John D. Calandra Italian American Institute
25 W. 43rd Street, 17th Floor
New York, NY 10036

CROSSINGS 28
ISBN 978-1-59954-169-3

TABLE OF CONTENTS

EDITOR AND TRANSLATOR'S NOTE

The name Amerigo Ruggiero and his book *Italiani in America* remain largely unknown outside the Italian-speaking academic world. Since its first publication in 1937, *Italiani in America* has never been reprinted in Italy nor translated into English, despite its being recognized as one of the most important studies on the Italian immigrant community in North America of its time.

In translating and editing this study, I have tried to remain as close as possible to Ruggiero's original prose. In order to preserve the historical context of the original, I have retained the general use of masculine pronouns and the racial, ethnic, and clinical references that today are considered inappropriate and derogatory. In the latter case, I have enclosed the term in quotation marks. I have also largely left in italics and and in quotation marks English words found in the source text. Some additional footnotes have been added to the target text where it may be of help to the reader.

I wish to express my appreciation to Florida State University for providing me with a sabbatical that facilitated greatly the completion of this project and to my graduate students who were generous readers of the manuscript in its early stages. My special thanks to Maria Andriulli, the President of the Associazione Mondi Lucani, and to Anthony Tamburri, Dean of the John D. Calandra Italian American Institute, for their unwavering support and hospitality, which have proven to be invaluable to my research on Amerigo Ruggiero and the Italian American community. A word of appreciation to Ortensio Ruggiero for his kindness in sharing with me helpful information and documentation related to his great uncle. I should also like to put on record my gratitude to the following for their encouragement and assistance in my research: Alberto Gallelli, Biblioteca Geografia e Nordamericana, Università degli Studi di Firenze, the Centro Lucani nel Mondo "Nino Calice," Professor Maria Raffaella Magistro, Filippo Luberto, mayor of Grassano, Giuseppe Disabato, Suditalia Video (Montescaglioso), and journalist Giovanni Spadafino. Many thanks to Bordighera Press, especially to Nicholas Grosso for his assistance and patience in the editorial process. A final expression of gratitude to my newfound friends at the Caffè Letterario of Montescaglioso and to Karen Myers for her continued aesthetic advice.

INTRODUCTION TO THE TRANSLATION[1]

In the introduction to his 2005 anthology on Italian American writings, *Italoamericana: Storia e letteratura degli italiani negli Stati Uniti 1880-1943*, Francesco Durante notes that Italian critics and scholars had long neglected, or ignored, the patrimony of Italian American culture as well as the complexity and variety of the Italian American question.[2] Durante is quick to point out that today the situation regarding studies on immigration has changed rather dramatically.[3] In fact, there has occurred for some time now a radical change in Italy's place on the stage of international migration. In his review of works on Italian Americans, Italian critic Goffredo Fofi writes that it is only relatively recently that Italian Americans became fashionable. They used to be of interest only when one of them was famous, either in films, politics, or sports, and only in those sports like baseball and boxing in which the rise to the top was particularly fierce.[4] Fofi adds that the Italian immigrants were once viewed from a distance with a mixture of smugness and amazement because to "real" Italians they did not appear to be one of them but rather they were considered a strange hybrid that had to do only with the most poor, the most wayward, and the most ignorant: the Southerners and peasants.

In his study *Voices of Italian America. A History of Early Italian American Literature*, Martino Marazzi addresses the question of a lack of attention given to the immigrant experience and its developments in the country of arrival by spokesmen for Italian culture. In chapter 7 titled "Italian Americans and Italian Writers," Marazzi begins with

---

1 Parts of this essay were published in Italian in the journal *Campi immaginabili. Rivista Semestrale di Cultura* under the title of "La 'passionata eloquenza' nel libro *Italiani in America* (1937) di Amerigo Ruggiero," 56/57, I/II, 2017: 486-502.

2 Francesco Durante, *Italo-Americano: Storia e letteratura degli italiani negli stati uniti 1880-1943*. (Milan, Mondadori, 2005): 4. English edition: *Italoamericana. The Literature of the Great Migration, 1880-1943*. Edited by Robert Viscusi (New York: Fordham University Press, 2014).

3 Durante, Ibid.

4 Goffredo Fofi, *Emigranti in carriera*, in "Il sole 24 ore," 13 March 2004, n. 335: 28.

a quote by Giose Rimanelli, author of the 'emigration' novels *Peccato originale* and *Una posizione sociale*, ("And then I don't even want to speak to you about Italian Americans, they're all raving mad"), which serves as a telling snapshot of a general reluctance by the Italian cultural mediators to dedicate due attention to the Italian American community.[5] Marazzi observes that the long-standing unease of the Italian intellectual toward another Italy plays a part in this apparent disregard. It is an Italy that is "so subordinate as to be far away, unknown at home, and not easily defined [...]" (139). Marazzi speaks of the "zero degree" of the relationship between the intellectual away from home and his distant Italian American cousin. In his 1936 volume *Atlante americano*, the antifascist writer and journalist Giuseppe Antonio Borgese, who had moved to the United States in 1931 for political reasons and where he would remain to teach at several American universities until 1948, observes that among all the tragedies that have affected the masses no one is greater and sadder than that of Italian immigration. And yet, Borgese indicates that "it is still a subject up for discussion among Italian writers if it is true that they are in search of issues that are both human and national."[6] An eloquent example of the general lack of attention on the part of Italian literature and the Italian cultural mediators toward a social phenomenon of such vast dimensions that affected in so many ways millions of Italians between 1880 to the late 1920s and beyond is the almost deafening silence of the famous Italian essayist and critic Emilio Cecchi, whose legendary travel book *America amara* cataloguing his journey to the United States between 1938 and 1939 made no mention of the world of emigration.[7] However, in his forward to the volume, Cecchi does attempt to justify his reasons for not dedicating any of his fifty-one chapters to his fellow countrymen by observing that it would have been impossible to do any better or any differently than what Amerigo Ruggiero had done in his 1937 book *Italiani in*

---

5   Martino Marazzi, *Voices of Italian America. A History of Early Italian Literature with a Critical Anthology*. Translated by Ann Goldstein. (Madison: Fairleigh Dickinson University Press, 2004): 292.

6   Giuseppe Antonio Borgese, *Atlante americano* (Modena: Guanda, 1931): 236.

7   Emilio Cecchi, *America amara* (Padua, Franco Muzzio Editore, 1995): 3.

America.[8] Cecchi adds that Ruggiero's work was one of his provisions for his "dreadful journey" to the United States. Ruggiero's *Italiani in America* is among the first comprehensive and authoritative studies of the Italian immigrant community in North America published in Italy.[9] In a Center for Migration Studies special issue on "The Italian in America before the Revolution," Giovanni Schiavo, a pioneering researcher on Italian Americans, referred to Amerigo Ruggiero as "the foremost correspondent of Italian newspapers in America" and to his book *Italiani in America* as "the most valuable single book on Italian immigration to the United States to this very day."[10] Despite the over eighty years that have passed since its publication, it remains, as Martino Marazzi has noted, "a model that lends itself to revival and should not be confined to the 1930s or to the multiple metamorphoses of anti-Americanism" produced during the height of Fascist Italy (Marazzi, 144). Marazzi's words are echoed by Franco Vitelli who, in recalling lines from Carlo Levi's *Christ Stopped at Eboli* that refer to Amerigo Ruggiero's notoriety as a journalist stationed in New York, writes that his *Italiani in America* "offers acute analyses that stand up to time, so much so to justify its republication."[11] Ruggiero's expertise as an

8   Amerigo Ruggiero, *Italiani in America* (Milan, Treves, 1937).

9   In her enlightening and wide-ranging book *The "Mito Americano" and Italian Literary Culture Under Fascism* (Rome: Aracne, 2015), Jane Dunnett refers to Ruggiero's *Italiani in America* as "the sole book devoted entirely to the question of emigration during the ventennio" (96). Also, Dunnett gives due credit to French scholar Michel Beynet, whose *L'image de l'Amèrique dans la culture italienne de l'entre-deux-guerres* (Aix-en-Provence: Publications de l'Université de Provence, 1990) addresses the long neglected Ruggiero's valuable contributions as a foreign correspondent in the USA and one of the most important cultural mediators between the United States and Italy during the 1930s. Dunnett writes: "Beynet is the only critic to do justice to this neglected figure, 'aujourd'hui à peu près complètement oublié,' recognising that 'il a été en son temps l'un des intermédiaires culturels les plus importants de l'Amérique en Italie.'" (397).

10   Giovanni Schiavo, "The Stupid Lie," *Special Issue: The Italian in America before the Revolution*, vol. 2, issue 1 (January 1976): 176.

11   I have translated the following lines from *Christ Stopped at Eboli* that Vitelli references: "The next day, I was invited to lunch by Mr. Orlando, the brother of a famous journalist who was living in New York [...] I had designed the cover of his brother's book on America [*L'America al bivio*]: this had been the pretext of

Americanist, who lived in the United States for many years, adds to the value of this work. Moreover, his volume raises questions relating to immigration, such as the reaction to a wave of immigration that ran counter to the Protestant, northern European roots on which "America's greatness" was founded, the treatment of "undesirable" and marginalized ethnic groups, and the unjustifiable deportation policies aimed at immigrants that are very much relevant today.

Amerigo Ruggiero was born in the southern Italian town of Grottole, located in the province of Matera, in 1878. At a young age, he moved with his family to the nearby town of Grassano. He received degrees in Medicine and Surgery and in Veterinary Science at the University of Naples Federico II. It was during his student years in Naples that Ruggiero became an activist in the Italian Socialist Party. His political militancy, which included his strongly anti-clerical writings, led to his arrest in Rome and imprisonment in Naples.[12] In 1907, at the age of twenty-nine, he immigrated to New York, where he joined his brother Amadeo, a licensed pharmacist, and where he began to collaborate with various newspapers and magazines. Following the outbreak of World War I, he first sided with the anti-interventionists but then decided to return to Italy and participate as a volunteer in the Alpini corps as a veterinary lieutenant. After practicing medicine for a few years near Rome, it was in his role as a foreign correspondent in the United States for the Turin newspaper *La Stampa* from 1929 to 1946 that gained him fame as a journalist. In an entry dedicated to Ruggiero from the biographical encyclopedia *Italiani di America*, edited by Ario Flamma, one reads: "In a New York Times article about journalism in Italy published in 1937, he [Ruggiero] was called the most read and most authoritative journalist of the peninsula."[13] Ruggiero's range and significant impact as a journalist are further highlighted in a brief biographical introduction when he joined the staff of *Divagando*,

---

our meeting [...]." Franco Vitelli, "Don Luigino recuperato. Primi documenti inediti e rari su Carlo Levi e la Lucania," *Forum Italicum*, vol. 50, n. 2 (2016): 391.

12   See Fabrizio Giulietti, *Storia degli anarchici italiani in età giolittiana* (Milano: Franco Angeli, 2012): 73-76.

13   Ario Flamma, ed. *Italiani di America* (New York: Casa Editrice Cocce Brothers, 1936): 296.

a weekly magazine in the Italian language published in New York for Italian American readers:

> For some weeks now, we have had as a member of our family Amerigo Ruggiero, the most prominent correspondent from New York for leading Italian newspapers and magazines [...] For over a quarter of a century, Ruggiero has drawn the attention of readers in Italy on what America has produced or is producing in every field of human knowledge: science, health, construction, literature, music, theater, and art. His articles have appeared almost daily in *La Stampa* of Turin, *Il Messagero* of Rome, *La Nazione* of Florence, *Il Giornale del Mezzogiorno*, *Il Mattino* of Naples, the *Giornale di Sicilia* and in other newspapers. Today, Ruggiero writes for the *Gazzetta del Popolo* of Turin. Among his many and varied journalistic pieces, we'd like to recall his inquiries on the technical, economic, and social development of the large Ford plants that were only superficially known in Italy. He revealed the most important details and the most vital aspects of that most typically American organization. We'd also like to recall the first-rate correspondence of his travels around America. Every different ethnic group was studied and described in its different characteristics of race and in relation to its contribution to the development of this great Republic and to the rapid assimilation to American life [...] Ruggiero is the author of a book published by Treves titled *Italiani d'America* [sic], considered the best study on the life and development of our immigrants [...].[14]

Even though Ruggiero's articles were predominantly on political, economic, and social topics in which the image of America that he presents is, as Marcello Ciocchetti has observed, largely one of "a nation in disarray, lacking in moral principles and socially fragmented," it is important to mention, if only briefly, his contributions on American literature.[15] In his writings for *La Stampa*, Ruggiero views American literature as a faithful reflection of its society and what he appreciates

---

14   *Divagando*, vol. xxiii (May 19, 1954): 10.

15   *La Stampa 1934-1945*. Edited by Marcello Ciocchetti. (Urbino: QuattroVenti, 1992): 16.

about its theater is precisely its ability to represent explicitly "the ugliness, the perversions, the decadence, and the failure of the model of the American way of life."[16] The authors that Ruggiero examines in his articles are those same writers who fostered the myth of America in the 1930s in Italy.[17] However, what distinguishes Ruggiero from other Americanists (e.g. Pavese, Pintor, Vittorini), writes Ciocchetti, is that he was perhaps the only one who had direct experience with American reality.

In his book *America amara. Storie e miti a stelle e strisce*, the historian Lucio Villari recalls that Mussolini, in an article for the fascist newspaper *Popolo d'Italia* on May 18, 1934, praised Ruggiero's reports from New York: "'They are not,' writes the Duce, 'colorful articles,' nor are they tall tales. They are articles drafted with a clear-sightedness and a straightforward telling of facts."[18] That same year Ruggiero published *L'America al bivio*, a penetrating glimpse into American life of the 1930s in which he traces the events following the stock market crash of 1929 through Roosevelt's recovery program of the New Deal.[19] In his study, Villari deals extensively with *L'America al bivio* in the hope that his comments will lead to the rediscovery and, consequently, to a re-reading of the Italian journalist's work "in order to better understand the ideal added value that was the intention of Roosevelt's *Brain Trust* […] and to stimulate a series of decisive social reforms."[20]

In addressing the subject of Italians in America, Ruggiero's longstanding interest in the political, moral, economic, and social

---

16   Ibid., 17.

17   Among those authors that Ruggiero examines are Sinclair Lewis, Theodore Dreiser, Erskine Caldwell, Sherwood Anderson, William Saroyan, and John Dos Passos. In her book *The "Mito Americano" and Italian Literary Culture Under Fascism*, Dunnett offers an overview of the articles Ruggiero dedicated to American literature, which appeared on the *terza pagina* of *La Stampa*. See section "5.4. Amerigo Ruggiero: Investigating the United States" in Dunnett's above-mentioned volume (397-404).

18   Lucio Villari, *America amara. Storie e miti a stelle e strisce.* (Rome: Salerno Editrice, 2013): 53.

19   Amerigo Ruggiero, *L'America al bivio.* (Turin: Einaudi, 1934).

20   Villari, 58.

problems of the Italian transoceanic emigration provides him with greater insight into the deficiencies and the neglect that impeded the development of the Italian communities abroad. Ruggiero anticipated the publication of his book on the Italian Americans with a series of articles that appeared in *La Stampa* in which he traced the long journey of the Italian immigrants to America during a period when "the Italian laborer, scorned and oppressed, contributed to forming the richness of the foreign lands."[21] He displays his expertise of the Italian American community in his article "Piccole Italie' oltre Oceano," as he offers a concise and vivid portrait of the "Little Italies" of New York from the Italian immigrants' early mass arrival to certain determined areas of the city where there resided groups of Europeans who had arrived immediately before them. Ruggiero notes that their settlement in these areas was not easy nor peaceful, particularly regarding their interactions with the "bullying" and "provocative" Irish. For these Italian immigrants, writes Ruggiero, their definitive settling down came at the cost of infinite tragedies: "our poor peasants from the South, without experience, without protection on the part of the native authorities and even less from representatives of their country, had to overcome with their own courage the right to live in a house and to be left in peace to work and tend to their own affairs."[22] Ruggiero describes in detail how the residents of the "Little Italies" sought to transplant as faithfully as possible the customs, traditions, atmosphere, and cuisine of their villages of origin. These colonies, he observes, recreate in general practices and lifestyles that are already long gone from their original villages. With the closure of immigration, Ruggiero indicates that the "Little Italies" have begun to disappear and that they no longer meet any need since the few Italians who now arrive are very different from past immigrants. Nevertheless, Ruggiero concludes, even though the "Little Italies" have lost their function, they represented for those who have lived in them for many years "an extension of the homeland" and they "helped to soften the bitterness of the separation and to sweeten

21   Amerigo Ruggiero, "Come erano e come sono gli Italiani d'America," *La Stampa* (26 November 1935): 3.

22   Amerigo Ruggiero, "Piccole Italie' oltre Oceano," *La Stampa* (20 May 1930):3.

the harshness of the environment."[23]

When Ruggiero's book appeared, the severity of judgment provoked a variety of reactions, such as the following review that was published in *La Stampa*:

> His [Ruggiero's] book could be cause for some distress and indignation, and justifiably so, because it has probed relentlessly all the implications and denounced all the faults, and because it has examined without compromise the pathos of a situation whose responsibility touches an entire class as well as the governments that preceded Fascism.[24]

The Preface by the General Director of Italians Abroad, Piero Parini, gives added value to Ruggiero's book.[25] Parini's admiration of Ruggiero's profound knowledge of the life of Italian Americans is immediately evident in the Preface's first paragraph:

> Only Amerigo Ruggiero could write this long-awaited book. Like few others he knows America and our communities. Like no other he has followed the events of our transoceanic emigration and has studied its problems in their infinite variety of political, economic, moral, and social characteristics. And like no other he loves those brothers of ours who have struggled long and hard to earn their little place in the sun.

Parini adds that Ruggiero's book presents "an ideal history of our country, or better yet of our people, from the Unification to the present day."

In his Introduction, Ruggiero sets out to offer with his book a general overview of what Italian immigration in North America has been, the transformations that it has undergone, and its future prospects.

---

23   Ibid., 3.

24   l.a.m. "La rivincita del 'cafone," *La Stampa* (15 June 1937): 3.

25   Ortensio Ruggiero, the great nephew of Amerigo Ruggiero, notes at the end of the Preface to his edition of *Italiani in America* that the famed journalist Mario Missiroli told him that he was in fact the author of the Preface. A photocopy of Ortensio Ruggiero's comment was sent to me by Maria Raffaella Magistro, Treasurer of the Association Mondi Lucani, on August 8, 2018.

Ruggiero boldly declares that the Italians, regretfully, were never seriously interested in the floods of people who left to enrich foreign lands. He speaks of an "olympic indifference" that characterized the Italians' relationship with the phenomenon of immigration particularly in the years preceding World War I. For many Italians, observes Ruggiero, "America was a place where a bunch of outcasts who, by some oddity of fate or environment, often succeeded in making a fortune." Ruggiero asserts that in general the act of emigration "was considered to be a sign of a derelict and the immigrant was looked at with masked scorn." He notes that unfortunately the emigration question began to be addressed seriously in Italy when there was no longer emigration; however, he adds, with a glowing sense of pride, that the fascist government had fueled a nearly extinguished flame of "Italianità" in the Italian colonies and had begun to clean up what had remained as a result of the disorganization of preceding years and to remedy the sad legacy of passed governments. Among the issues Ruggiero felt the need to explain to his readers in Italy, who would have had difficulty in understanding the conditions of the Italian community abroad, were the following: 1) given the original make-up of the Italian communities in America, they have little or no influence on American life. As a result of the low or non-existent literacy level of the Italian communities, many cultural initiatives ran aground leaving their promoters with no other option but to return to Italy discouraged and frustrated; 2) why Italian books and newspapers never had a successful distribution rate among the Italian colonies in America; and 3) how Italian theatrical companies of all kinds, after triumphant tours in South America, having arrived in New York, where they expected even greater triumphs, were compelled to disband after disastrous results. Ruggiero states that very few cultural figures, be they performing artists or visiting lecturers, shared what they really saw and encountered during their American experience. The reasons for this reluctance, he suggests, is because very few were willing to recognize that the springboard of culture could not be found among the old Italian immigrant communities who simply did not have any culture and "[if] they read books, they are along the lines of *Reali di*

Francia [The Royal House of France],[26] and if they go to the theater, it is to see works like *Iena del Cimitero* [The Hyena of the Cemetery][27] or *Mafiusi della Vicaria* [Heroes of the Penitentiary]. [28]

In an essay on the Italian book in America, Giuseppe Prezzolini, perhaps the most outspoken of the Italian intellectuals on the subject of Italian Americana and who served as director of the Casa Italiana of Columbia University from 1930 to 1940, reminds his readers that millions of Italian immigrants had come from rural areas where illiteracy was much higher, reaching levels of eighty or ninety per cent among those above six years of age.[29] He adds that the majority of these immigrants were never Italians in terms of language and never belonged to the Italian literary spirit. Even if they were able to read Italian, he continues, they would find very little to impassion them, for much of it would be tedious, unbearable, and incomprehensible. Prezzolini further indicates that a large portion of Italian books reflect the feelings, customs, habits, and hopes of the Italian middle class. The Italian American immigrants were not, he concludes, from this class; rather, they moved from a rural and agricultural civilization to an industrial, mechanical environment in America. In commenting on the books sold among the Italian American community in New York, Prezzolini writes: "In terms of Italian literature, the New York that speaks Italian is equivalent to a small provincial town in southern Italy that does not even have a train station. The level is much lower than one would find at a newsstand."[30] A similar perspective of the Italian American community is shared by Mario Einaudi who in the immediate post war years joined the Cornell University faculty and also served as a literary scout for Einaudi Publishers, founded by his brother Giulio. In a letter of 13 October 1945, Mario Einaudi responds

---

26   A prose chivalric romance written by Andrea da Barberino (1370-1431). The stories remained a part of the repertoire of puppet shows in Sicily.

27   A popular theatrical work among the Italian American community that was part of repertoire of plays by Antonio Maiori.

28   A play by Giuseppe Rizzuto first published in 1862 and performed in Sicily in 1863.

29   Giuseppe Prezzolini, *America in pantofole* (Florence: Vallecchi, 2002): 235.

30   Ibid, 238.

to his brother's request to explore the Italian American community as a possible target audience for the publishing house: "Here in the United States the Italian Americans are incurably illiterate and don't go beyond the level of Carolina Invernizio."[31]

The Italian roots of a large number of the most notorious gangsters in the United States prompted an exchange of letters between the young Cesare Pavese, a blossoming Americanist and one of the future founders of the Einaudi publishing firm, and his Italian America musician friend Anthony Chiuminatto who was originally from near the northern city of Turin and was now living in a gangster-infested Chicago. In a letter of 22 September 1930, Pavese's observations, encouraging his friend to take advantage of his Italian American heritage in order to have a better perspective on the two nations, allow the Italian question between the North and the South to cross borders into the United States and, at the same time, highlight a lack of understanding, or indifference, of the Italian intellectual to the perception of the Italian Americans in the new world:

> And you, who are in the tremendous situation of being both an Italian and an American, you must try to comprehend the two nations, try to raise above the petty difficulties. Moreover you must not forget that we Italians are two distinct nations, the North and the South, and that we are the Northern and that the Chicagoans gunmen are the Southern and there is a deeper difference of race and history between us and them that nothing can repair.[32]

In his response on 7 October 1930, Chiuminatto gives Pavese a brief lesson of the perception of Italian Americans in America:

> It's all well and good for you to remind me that Italians are distinctly in two classes, the Northern and the Southern.

---

31   Carolina Invernizio (1858-1916) was a novelist, who had a large popular success in Italy between the late 1800s and the early 20th century. The unpublished letter is found in the Mario Einaudi file of Einaudi Archive at the Turin Archivio di Stato.

32   Mark Pietralunga, ed., *Cesare Pavese & Anthony Chiuminatto: Their Correspondence* (Toronto: University of Toronto Press, 2007): 99-100.

But who the hell knows that but us Italians and about 10%
of the Americans? The general conception of the Italian in
America is based on the Sicilian make-up. Being an Italian in
Chicago to-day is not so pleasant; people look at you askance
when they know you are Italian, as much as to say, look out!
And the general run of America will tell you that they are
afraid of Italians, that they would not even rent rooms to an
Italian. How do you like that, eh?[33]

In his attempt to rectify the lack of support and disdain of the Italian
American communities by his fellow Italians in Italy, Ruggiero turns
his focus almost exclusively to the immigration from southern Italy,
since it has conferred a special distinction - be it tragic, picturesque,
shameful, or laudable- on the entire Italian immigration of North
America. Obviously, as mentioned above, the Italian immigrants'
illiteracy played an important role of the perception and lack of respect
towards them. Much earlier, in 1902, Gherardo Ferrari, in his book
Gli italiani in America: impressioni di un viaggio agli stati uniti, had
noted that the "Italian name could never be appreciated in the United
States as long as it was represented by illiterate immigrants whom the
Americans compared to 'leeches stuck to the legs of a Hippogriff.'"[34]

In his harsh treatment of a materialistic and fragile American society,
Ruggiero offers the following description of the Italian Americans:

[...] upon first contact with the Italian Americans and
their condition, there immediately surfaces in the mind of
someone who has freshly arrived from Italy an extremely
intense antipathy. The young Italian Americans use a jargon
to define the various types of Italians with whom they come
into contact. The descriptions are far from flattering: generally
they are ridiculous and crass. Italians find the descendants of
their compatriots crude, uneducated, ignorant, and intolerable.
They lack refinement, they do not know how to converse,
they do not respect their elders, and with the exception of
baseball and cars they're not interested in anything.

---

33   Ibid., 104.

34   Gherardo Ferreri, *Gli italiani in America: impressioni di un viaggio agli Stati
Uniti* (Rome: Tipografia del Campidoglio di G. D'Antonis, 1907): 14.

For Ruggiero, the real tragedy of the Italian American is that they are neither fish nor fowl, lacking the respect of both their new and old societies. The Italian American, according to Ruggiero, "is not loved by those of his race and is given little consideration by the society of which he has become a part." He adds that the Italian American does not belong to either world, since "he is a hybrid, a grafting that often succeeds, but many times fails badly."

A similar, and perhaps even harsher, perspective of the Italian Americans is offered by the 29 year-old writer and journalist Mario Soldati who in 1935 published his views of the United States in the popular and often reprinted work *America primo amore* (*America First Love*), which is a collection of articles that appeared in various literary reviews in Italy between 1929 and 1934.[35] Soldati's volume is an account of his experience during his two-year stay between 1929 and 1931 in America as a result of receiving a fellowship from Columbia University. He would return two years later but for a shorter stay. Soldati's initial reaction is one of fascination for the novelty of the country, its material advancements and prosperity, and the striking modes of social interaction. The author compares his experiences to those of the first immigrants to America. As his journey continues, however, Soldati becomes progressively disillusioned by the 'spiritual barbarity' of the American society. In his review of *America primo amore*, Prezzolini writes that it was "openly hostile to America, full of antipathy, disgust, and ridicule, as much as from an irritated sensibility to the smells and colors of America as from an intelligence annoyed by American values."[36] And with particular reference to Soldati's feelings towards the Italian Americans, Prezzolini observes: "he cares least of all for the Italian Americans."[37] Soldati's aversion toward the Italian Americans is best depicted in a chapter dedicated to the Costantinos, an Italian family who lives in the Bronx and who is presented as the

---

35   Mario Soldati, *America primo amore* (Florence: Bemporad, 1935). Quotes are from edition published by Sellerio (Palermo) in 2003. Translations are mine.

36   Giuseppe Prezzolini, "Quelli che ci vogliono bene," in *La Settimana* (17 January 1936): 13.

37   Ibid.

prototype of the Italian American family. Before he arrives at the home of the Costantino family, Soldati reflects on the dreary decadence and spiritual poverty that distinguishes the Italian Americans from their native civilization. He expresses his surprise over "those manners of a new moneyed country bumpkin, those dull conversations, that noisy and conventional joviality: the arrogance of belonging to a very rich and noble nation, and their disdain toward whoever is not a citizen" (Soldati, 57-58). Soldati observes that these shortcomings were especially conspicuous in the Italian Americans of the second generation: "Frightening was the obvious disgust of these young Italo Americans towards their parents who, having immigrated, had given them that prosperity in which they deluded themselves and the nationality of which they were so proud" (58). Just a few weeks after his arrival in New York, the initial, naïve respect Soldati held for the Italian Americans quickly disappears. The invitation from the Costantino family was received with great joy and high expectations on the part of Soldati who was eager to make acquaintances in his adopted country. The journey to the Costantino's residence on Humboldt Avenue in the Bronx was the complete opposite of what he had imagined and is a harbinger for things to come: "Hearing the name Humboldt I imagined either a long and extensive boulevard, with villas surrounded by English style gardens and lawns; or luxurious high rises with all the comforts much like one finds along Park Avenue" (61). Instead, Soldati found himself among vast, bleak, maze-like streets surrounded by walls of billboard signs, dumpsites and factory smokestacks. In the midst of all this were entire neighborhoods of gray houses, built in cement or wood, that were all identical, each with a small front porch, surrounded by a few feet of grass, and each with an adjacent shack for a Ford or a Chevrolet. These residential neighborhoods were inhabited by immigrants who had fully become participants in the American way of life. Soldati describes the sounds that emerge from the home as he approaches the front porch: "Mr. and Mrs. Constantino, in anticipation of their guest who was fresh off the boat from Italy, were preparing to welcome him by recharging with the old phonograph the old Italian atmosphere: that air of Angloamerican Italy of 'O Sole Mio' or 'Torna a Surriento' that never left us and continued to torment us the moment we stepped foot out of Italy" (62-63).

The Costantinos, whose Italianness consists of these songs, are short, fat, crass and greasy. They have five or six children between ten and twenty years of of age who laugh at their guest and constantly repeat as a compliment that he is a "green horn" while, at the same time, expressing the joy of feeling themselves "American citizens." For Soldati, the Costantinos, like other immigrants of the nineteenth and twentieth centuries, are "cut off from America as they are from Italy" and represent "the mentality of a barber from Catania around 1890" or "the provincial and middle-class society of Avellino, Aquila, Benevento, or Potenza, etc. before the war" (65). Their wine is disgusting and their food is tasteless and a bad copy of the Italian original, while they are extremely proud of "that kilo of paper that is the Sunday newspaper."

Just a few years before Soldati narrates his American experiences in *America primo amore*, another well-educated, northern Italian, Luigi Barzini Jr., immigrated to the United States in 1925 where he would remain until his graduation in 1930. In his autobiography *O America, When You and I Were Young*, Barzini Jr. writes about his experiences during his student days at the City College of New York:

> For some reason, I found the Jews more interesting than the boys of Italian blood. The Italians had shed what little *italianità* their parents had brought to the new country, and did not speak a word of the language, not even their original patois. They knew nothing about Italy, in fact, little more than what they had been told in the American schools, and, as a result, were somewhat embarrassed by their origins and their names. The Jews, with their hunger for books and ideas, their wit, their capacity to spin webs of ingenious arguments, their compassion, their acceptance of reality and the nature of man, were nearer to me. It was easier to talk to them.[38]

As Anthony Tamburri has noted, there are a number of basic issues that come into play in this passage. First, there is the question of

---

38   Luigi Barzini, *O America When You and I Were Young* (New York: Harper & Row Publishers, 1977): 93.

"ethnic retention."[39] "The Italian boys," writes Tamburri, shed their *italianità* and, in so doing, lose their parents' language, Italian, as well as the local *patois*, "Italglish" or "Italese," as it is sometimes called (Tamburri, 61). In addition, we also read that they know very little to nothing of Italy, only what they learned in school, and, as a result, are embarrassed because of it. Though a clear dichotomy is established between the Italian Americans and the Jews, what interests us here, continues Tamburri, is the dichotomy between Barzini and the Italian Americans. Here socio-economics underscores this difference, as Barzini comes from a family of the college-educated whereas the Italians he met at college were predominantly first-generation college students. Tamburri offers an interesting parallel between Barzini's relationship with Italian Americans in 1926 and what we see today in various parts of of Italian America. He indicates that many children and grandchildren of Italian immigrants have no knowledge of Italian history and whether its government is parliamentary or presidential. Tamburri then adds that "they are linguistically challenged, unable to access directly Italian culture because they cannot negotiate adequately in Italian" and, consequently, "the ability to engage in nuance, implication, and intimation falls by the wayside; and communication, at best, is reduced to rudimentary practices" (63). Tamburri asserts that, by and large, the Italian Americans "have little interest in cultural things Italian (read, Italian and Italian/American); or, one might presume, their linguistic shortcoming actually constitutes an inability for them to acquire that knowledge that would stimulate interest" (63). Tamburri offers the following example to make his point:

> [...] given the plethora of cultural activities that take place, for instance within the greater New York area, it is intriguing, to be sure, that the representatives—be they leaders or general members—of the so-called power-broking, Italian and Italian/American organizations do not attend in the numbers one might expect, especially since they are given such conspicuous roles. (63)

---

39 Anthony Tamburri, *Re-Reading Italian Americana: Specificities and Generalities on Literature and Criticism* (Teaneck: Fairleigh Dickenson University Press, 2014): 61.

As has been highlighted above, Prezzolini was not one to mince words as he considered the Italian community, particularly in and around the New York area, as a distorted version of Italian but not yet Americans. Prezzolini expressly stated that the Italian Americans' jargon was insufficient as a language of culture and that the Italian Americans served as an obstacle in the promotion of Italian culture, language, and literature in the United States. With regard to this last point, we might recall Prezzolini's comments in reference to the relations between the Casa Italiana at Columbia University and the Italian American community:

> The Casa was made possible by the generosity of the community but as a concept it was above their intellectual reach. The average italo-american never comprehended what the Casa really stood for… The Casa must be a center of relations between the real Italy and the real U.S. It has been my conviction that for these relations the Italian community here was a stumbling block rather than a bridge.[40]

According to Prezzolini, the Italians in America are no longer Italians but they are not yet Americans: "[A]nd this hybrid, transitory, and ambiguous situation in which the Italian Americans find themselves is the result of fifty years of shame, sufferings, hard work, and sacrifice, that some extraordinary achievements were not enough to bury and to forget."[41] Prezzolini argued that if the Italian Americans wanted to be that bridge between the two countries they needed to be more united, more focused in their aims, and more respectful of the values of culture. Nevertheless, Prezzolini goes on to contend that Italians, who have given entire generations to America and have left their blood and sweat throughout the country and to whom roads, railroads, buildings, and important social changes are owed, figure much less prominently in the history of the United States than do the French, whose only participation was limited to several thousand soldiers and

40   Giuseppe Prezzolini and Daria Frezza Bicocchi, "A proposito di Casa Italiana alla Columbia University e di fascismo, *Studi Storici*, 12, 2 (April - June, 1971): 417.

41   Prezzolini, *America in pantofole*: 207.

a general for purely nationalistic and selfish reasons (208). However, continues Prezzolini, in the United States everyone doffs their cap to the name of La Fayette, yet they remain silent when speaking of Italian immigration. Prezzolini holds Ruggiero's volume in high esteem as he considers it a "retaliation" of the Italians in America against the twofold misunderstanding by the Italians in Italy and by the Americans in the United States:

> Amerigo Ruggiero in a beautiful, courageous, honest, loving, and fast-paced book, goes directly to its objective, and, as a consequence, often takes the short cut of simplification: no statistics, no names, few anecdotes or small facts; nevertheless, it carries you along from page to page, and captivates you with his brutal analysis, his sharp vision, his harsh reasoning, and his passionate eloquence. (208)

Prezzolini then focuses on what he deems to be the most original part of Ruggiero's book, namely that aspect of Italian immigration that had been neglected and scorned previously and subsequently. He calls into question the figure of the *cafone*, the southern peasant, that Italian "who is short in stature, whose skin is the color of terracotta, whose pace is slow, and whose demeanor is rough, suspicious, ignorant, and ungrateful" (208). And yet, it is to this figure that much of what the Italians had done well in America is owed:

> Abandoned by his own country that did not provide him with schooling or social protection, neglected by consular authorities, exploited by the *galantuomo*, that is by the southern petty bourgeoisie, in his reincarnation as exchange broker, notary public, lawyer and politician, he [the *cafone*] has discovered alone the road to redemption by leaving his homeland, immigrating to distant lands, enduring the scorn and the slavery-like treatment of his new masters. He has learned the language without going to school, saving at the cost of immense sacrifices, and finding a solution for his own destiny as well as to that of his country. (208-209)

After highlighting the adaptation process and the many successes of the *cafone* in America, Ruggiero turns his attention to the so-called *galantuomini.*[42] The latter, contrary to the *cafoni*, do not possess the gifts of adaptability and versatility or an open and tolerant disposition that allow them to accept very different aspects and systems of life. Consequently, what the immigrant petty bourgeoisie lacks is "a sense of perspective and historical understanding." In other words, the *galantuomini* "should have immigrated to America with a pioneering spirit, without deluding themselves into believing they could find a social system that would protect them." Instead, besides not having the spirit or the physique of a pioneer, they had the added handicap of not knowing the language. For Ruggiero, their inadaptability to the new customs and environment and their inability to learn the language and adapt to different ideas and manners resulted in the Americans labeling all Italians as "unassimilable" during the debate concerning the anti-immigration law:

> The Americans judged an entire Italian population by a class that, in its own country of origin, was in a state of distress and represented only the remnants of a Middle Ages that lingered on in the South longer than in any other place. They labeled the Italians as *unassimilable*. It was one of the most serious indictments when the famous law against immigration was debated. The *unassimilability* of the Italians became axiomatic.

Ruggiero does not hesitate to assert that there is even something worse for the *galantuomo* than counting less than the *cafone*:

> [The *galantuomo*] absolutely needed him [the *cafone*]. Without the *cafone* the immigrant *galantuomo* would have found himself in the condition of a new-born child. He could have been in a state of despair due to hunger and cold in the gutter of a street and no one would have noticed. It was the *cafone* who took him by hand at his arrival, guided him, gave him the first instructions, and put in his head the first ideas of how

---

42   Franco Vitelli points out that a novelty of Ruggiero's book is that the relationship between the *cafoni* and the *galantuomini* is not only examined in southern Italy but also in places of expatriation, and with the recognition of the former's superiority over the latter as a result of a more lively and open aptitude to adapt to new situations. Vitelli, "Don Luigino recuperato": 392.

to live and manage in his adopted country, and... fed him.

Prezzolini recognizes that Ruggiero's book sheds light on the incomparable merits of these southern immigrants with such vivid details that only someone living in America could appreciate their true value. Prezzolini is also drawn to Ruggiero's focus on these immigrants' contribution to the diet and health of the Americans, which no one had really treated before in such detail. With regard to their diet, Ruggiero noted that as recently as twenty years earlier the Americans ate very badly. There was an incredible abuse of meat, which they ate as much as three times a day, while vegetables and legumes were virtually absent.

> Their cuisine was crude, primitive, and lacking in taste and flavor: a pioneer cuisine. One can imagine the effects of such a one-dimensional and little varied diet. The Americans suffered from dyspepsia, constipation, kidney and heart problems, and high blood pressure. One of the most glaring effects of such an unwise diet was their very bad teeth.

As Simone Cinotto has observed, Ruggiero maintained that an improvement in diet had significant consequences on the physical traits of the new generations of Italian Americans of New York.[43] Cinotto quotes a lengthy passage from *Italiani in America* that highlights the changes that occur as result of the defeat of hunger on the part of the immigrants and their access to a more rich and varied diet that contributed to "fill the void, as much physiological as social and cultural, on which the discrimination that plagued them first in Italy and then in the United States was based" (Cinotto, 158). Ruggiero notes that the Italian immigrants and their children, especially those coming from the southern regions, "had suffered and were suffering from different organic difficiencies than those that afflicted Americans" (158). While the Americans, writes Ruggiero, abused a meat diet and rarely ate vegetetables, fruits, and legumes, the Italian immigrants did the complete opposite by consuming an abundance of vegetable,

---

43   Simone Cinotto, *Una famiglia che mangia insieme: Cibo ed etnicità nella comunità italoamericana di New York, 1920-1940* (Turin: Otto Editore, 2001): 158.

fruits, and legumes and used much less frequently meat, milk, and butter. Compounded with the lack of vitamins, both in Italy and America, the result was often a case of rickets. Ruggiero observes that this tendency toward rickets carried with it the humiliation of seeing in American scientific studies Italians classified alongside the blacks. Moreover, he adds, the dietary deficiency impacted profoundly the skeletal development producing the short stature of those populations: "It was that small stature and the pitiful appearance that so negatively impressed the Americans who ended up considering us a degenerate race, corrupted by organic defects that would have never allowed it to develop an advanced civilization." Ruggiero does wish to point out that there are clear indications to be found in America that this deficiency in height is not a fixed characteristic of one's race:

> Certain things seem almost miraculous among those immigrants who, thanks to their more fortunate economic conditions and sharper intelligence, have been able to raise children in homes full of space, light, and air, in clean and sanitary neighborhoods, by feeding them rationally during their developmental years and, following the example of the Americans, by using plenty of milk and butter, while not forgetting classic Italian foods, and by having them take advantage of sports. Giants have emerged from shrunken, almost dwarf-like parents.

Furthermore, adds Ruggiero, another trait that begins to fade in America is the dark skin color of the Southerners confirming, in his opinion, that it was a result of climactic conditions: "Their children, who are born in America, have much fairer skin than their ancestors."

In the chapter "The Second Generation," Ruggiero offers an unflattering portrait of the new generation of Italian Americans, particularly the large majority that comes from the slums. He writes that the new generation "hate[s] everything that is Italian or smells Italian" and for them Italy "represents the poverty and the coarseness of their parents, which is reflected in their current state." And the physical appearance of these descendants of immigrants do not resemble in any way the descendants of the more fortunate immigrants mentioned previously:

> Little, deformed, and with putrid teeth, they wear on their face
> the imprint of brutality and degeneration. The girls as much
> as the boys. They congregate on corners and their shouts and
> husky voices make you shudder. They remind you of hardened
> escaped prisoners. They speak a kind of *babu english*, as they
> say in India about the English spoken by Indians, and their
> vocabulary does not exceed two hundred words. They look
> stupid and are prone to insults and threats. Their intelligence
> has remained atrophied, as have their feelings. They have no
> affection for anyone, they feel no sense of obligation toward
> anyone, and they do not respect or obey anyone. They fear
> only the laws of the *gang*: it is their book of law. If their
> parents had remained in Italy, they would have become
> honest peasants and expert artisans. Here they will become
> criminals, *gangsters*, and subject to hanging.

Ruggiero recognizes that "[n]umerous and brilliant exceptions do
exist" but, he quickly adds, they are not sufficient enough to change a
situation that can only be remedied over time. According to Ruggiero,
if the descendants of immigrants have struggled in making inroads
in the economic world, it is even worse in the social world. Ruggiero
concludes his chapter on the second generation by summarizing what
he believes to be the tragedy of the Italian Americans and stating
that, in the end, very few will sow seeds of prosperity, which will be
a testament to the vitality of the Italian race:

> The tragedy of the Italo-Americans is that of all *déracinés*, of
> all those who have been torn from their original stock and
> transplanted in a new land, in a new environment among
> new human groups. Many are disheartened and become lost,
> others, perhaps the majority, settle in with difficulty and lead
> a miserable and painful life. Only those few gifted at birth
> with admirable and vital energies and spiritual and physical
> qualities that put them in a position to adapt, without great
> effort or serious handicaps, to the necessities of an existence
> quite different from those of their ancestors will plant powerful
> roots in the soil. These will give life to the majestic trunk that
> will remain as testimony to the strength of a race.

In the months preceding the publication of *Italiani in America*, Ruggiero published large parts of this chapter on the second generation of Italian Americans in two separate installments of the periodical *La Settimana*. The weekly was founded by the honorable Edward Corsi, a distinguished political and intellectual figure in the Italian community of New York.[44] *La Settimana*'s managing editor was the one and the same Amerigo Ruggiero and its contributors included some of the most well-known names in Italian journalism and culture in New York, from the above mentioned Prezzolini to Beniamino De Ritis,[45] from Alfonso Arbib-Costa[46] to Angelo Patri.[47] In an essay for the journal *La Stirpe* published in 1930, Ruggiero had revealed himself to be an attentive observer of the new forms of communication and

44   Edward Corsi served as Director of the Haarlam House settlement from 1926 to 1931 and was then nominated by President Herbert Hoover to the office of United States Commissioner of Immigration and Naturalization at Ellis Island, which he held from 1931 to 1933. In 1934 New York Mayor Fiorello La Guardia nominated him to be the Director of the Home Relief Fund. Corsi would later become Deputy Commissioner for the New York City Department of Public Welfare. In 1935 he wrote the memoir *In the Shadow of Liberty: The Chronicle of Ellis Island* (New York: Macmillan).

45   Beniamino De Ritis was one of Italy's leading journalists, who served as correspondent in the United States and other parts of the world for a number of Italian newspapers. His publications include *La terza America* (Florence: Sansoni, 1937), *Stati Uniti dalla guerra civile al nuovo trattamento* (Milan: Istituto per gli Studi di Politica Internazionale, 1938), *Mente puritano in corpo pagano* (Florence: Valecchi, 1934).

46   Alfonso Arbib-Costa was a journalist and instructor in Romance Languages at New York University. From 1918 to 1919 he was one of the directors of the Italian Bureau of Information. His publications include *Italian Lessons* (New York: Italian Book Company, 1917) and *Advanced Italian Lessons* (New York: Italian Book Company, 1924).

47   Angelo Patri was the first Italian American public school administrator in the United States. From 1908 to 1913 he was principal of Public School No. 4 and in 1913 he became principal of Public School 45 in the Bronx, where he implemented an approach influenced by John Dewey's *Ethical Principles Underlying Education*. His publications include *A Schoolmaster of the Great City* (New York, Macmillan, 1917), *Child Training* (New York: Appleton, 1922), and *The Questioning Child and Other Essays* (New York: Appleton, 1931).

new means of popular entertainment like motion pictures, jazz, and detective novels.[48] He writes that in a dynamic nation like America, where there existed extreme class mobility, the creation of a diverse, mass culture that had taken place was a sign of the advent of the masses on the social scene. Consequently, it was almost irrelevant to ask if the new cultural productions like motion pictures were at the same level as the preceding ones. He stressed that it was important to create a culture that is in harmony with our times. This is precisely what the opening essay in the first issue of *La Settimana*, published on December 27, 1935 and penned by a certain "Venerdi," sought to articulate: "The world is tired and old, eaten away by a long series of chronic and perhaps incurable ills. With all this, the editors remain firm in their conviction that the path forward is an eminently fascinating one and it is with this spirit and this conviction that they will observe things and they will present, week by week, a clear motion picture of the events and of mankind."[49] Ruggiero and Edward Corsi fully understood that the Italian immigrants had been kept in conditions of inferiority as a result of their humble social state. At the same time, the magazine's editors noted that there were some encouraging signs concerning Italian life in America. Above all, the editorial staff of *La Settimana* was committed to bringing into the world, the homes, and the activities of its readers a reflection of the Italian immigrant life in the most familiar, human and concrete terms as possible. When they stated Italians in America, their intention was not to speak to any specific individuals, to intellectuals or to the privileged but rather to the vast majority spread out across the country: "to the unknown, to the laborers, to the diggers, to the unsung and silent sentries who heroically dug the trenches of the American civilization." As for art and culture, the editors of *La Settimana* were eager to accept all types of works provided that they were "heartfelt and sincere, inspired and built on an idea" and that they captured the character of the Italian American and the figure of the immigrant because no character, "is more worthy to be contained in pages of passion and torment."

The first installment of Ruggiero's piece on the second generation

48 Amerigo Ruggiero, "La crisi di una cultura," *La Stirpe* (December 1930): 514.

49 Venerdi, "Settimana per settimana" (27 December 1935): 3.

of Italians in America was published in the January 31, 1937 issue of *La Settimana*, with the second and final installment appearing in the subsequent edition of the weekly on February 7, 1937. The title of the first article, "The Second Generation," is accompanied by the following statement/disclaimer: "These observations are not intended to cast any contempt or discredit on the descendants of our people who arrived on American soil." Seemingly by chance—so the editors affirm—and unbeknownst to the respective authors, one finds in the January 31 issue of *La Settimana*, which contains Ruggiero's unflattering portrait of the second generation of Italian Americans, Edward Corsi's lead article about the many accomplishments of the young Italian Americans in all fields.[50] Corsi begins by speaking of his own personal experience as a university student when one of his professors announced in front of the entire class that if he had the authority he would prohibit all the young offspring of immigrant parents from occupying public offices of responsibility. According to Corsi, his professor did not believe that these youths had the steadiness, loyalty, and sense of duty required of people who held such positions. Corsi was particularly pained by the conviction expressed in his professor's "voice, eyes, and thought." In his article, Corsi seeks to respond with facts in an attempt to prove as unjustified the apparent general opinion that this young generation of Italian Americans represents a serious problem and an actual social threat. He notes that one of the most encouraging signs concerning Italian life in America is the progress made by the young generation. Having started out with nothing, alone, without inherited wealth or culture, without any backing or social prestige, this legion of promising and fresh intelligence, according to Corsi, is climbing the social ladder most admirably and impressively. In New York alone, he points out, there are 2000 teachers, 2500 social workers, 1000 lawyers, 1000 doctors and hundreds of others in the fields of engineering and architecture, in the arts, business and in the banking world. After dismissing the prejudices and accusations of being incapable of any serious and significant responsibilities, he writes: "with very few and negligible exceptions, the Italians, who were elected

---

50   Edward Corsi, "I giorni – Gli eventi – Le cose," *La Settimana* (31 January 1937): 3.

to public offices or chosen to serve in positions of high authority in business, always demonstrated an honorable conduct and always left behind works worthy of admiration" (3). Corsi presents a list of men of unparalleled moral and political integrity who have emerged from this new generation of Italian Americans. They include chief consul to the US Senate Committee on Banking and Currency Ferdinand Pecora, New York Mayor Fiorello La Guardia, Superior and Supreme Court Justice of Rhode Island Antonio Capotosto, Attorney General of Pennsylvania Walter Alessandroni, and Justice of the New York State Supreme Court Salvatore Cotillo. Despite the young Italians being pioneers in the fields in which they are making inroads, Corsi points out that they are often expected to achieve higher qualities than their rivals from other ethnic groups. Consequently, they must face the harsh prejudice that only heralds their defeat even before they have had the opportunity to succeed. Corsi sadly admits that this prejudice is not only found among those of past immigrations but also among the Italians themselves:

> Rarely does a young man find in our communities his talent appropriately appreciated if he is not first judged and recognized by the great mass of the American people [...] This is particularly true in the professional field. Many brave and brilliant lawyers cannot pay rent while our merchants employ in their business lawyers of other nationalities whose only merit is that they are not Italian. The same can be said for young Italian American physicians who must await the baptism of Americans to receive any attention and respect even in the communities where they were born. (3)

In the subsequent issues of *La Settimana*, Corsi's article on the Italian American youth and his recognition of its character, ingenuity, and awareness of human values, along with a fearlessness of competition, continued to be applauded by the weekly's readers and prominent Italian American leaders. On the other hand, Ruggiero's articles on the second generation of Italians in America elicited a much more negative response from the weekly's readership. One of these negative reactions came from the aforementioned Supreme Court Justice

Salvatore Cotillo who published in the February 14, 1937 issue of *La Settimana* an article titled "Cotillo on the Second Generation: What we need is a realization of the facts and not just criticism." As the title suggests, Cotillo is particularly critical of Ruggiero's approach of listing the weaknesses of the younger generation of Italian Americans while failing to do justice to their strengths. Despite recognizing that there are a good many criminals of this younger generation and many have failed to keep pace with the vast majority who have escaped the slums and the tenements, Cotillo indicates that the district he represented in the Senate and the State Assembly gave to the city men of character and quality like Fiorello La Guardia, Edward Corsi, Angelo Patri, Leonard Covello,[51] and recognized leaders in the fields of public service, education, business, and other professional activities who could serve as models for their community. Cotillo expresses his agreement with Commissioner Corsi, when the latter declared in his article for *La Settimana* that we often fail to see the forest because of the trees, claiming that too little is said about the many who are worthwhile and too much of the few who are "bad, dim-witted, and irresponsible." Cotillo then addresses Ruggiero's questioning of the Italianism of the younger Italian American men and women: "I agree that they are incapable of that demonstrativeness which characterizes the patriotic demonstrations of our older generation but behind their seeming indifference is a loyalty to blood and race which is not surpassed by the showy flag waving of our colonial orators" (15). He asserts that the time has come to do justice to the second generation. Keeping in mind the obstacles that the children of immigrants had to contend with, Cotillo argues that they have performed miracles beyond any expectation, bringing honor to themselves and to their race. Cotillo concludes by calling for a realization of the facts, a true picture of what the sons and daughters of immigrants have accomplished in America and not appraisals and criticism that, however applicable twenty and

---

51   Leonard Covello was an innovative public school teacher and administrator. In 1934 he founded and became principal of Benjamin Franklin High School in East Harlem, one of the centers of Italian immigration. His publications include *The Heart is the Teacher* (New York: McGraw Hill, 1958), and *The Social Background of the Italo-American School Child* (Leiden: Brill, 1967).

thirty years previously, were certainly misleading in the 1930s.

In response to Cotillo and to the many other readers who wrote *La Settimana* about his harsh analysis of the Italian American community, Ruggiero sends the following letter to the weekly's editor that by no means calms the heated debate:

> Dear Editor: the recent publication of my book *Italiani in America* with Casa Treves Publishers has provoked various comments. Naturally, it was not well received by those who recognized themselves in the book. Honorable Corsi's now famous list of noteworthy figures of the our Italian communities has proven to be quite timely. This list is, in a certain sense, the best and most definitive comment about the book.
>
> In essence, the Italian communities in America after 60 or 70 years of existence cannot offer any other list of noteworthy people than the one presented by the Honorable Corsi. And this is said with the utmost respect for those names included on the list. There are many who are content with these names and a contented mind is a continual feast. Let us add that the Kingdom of God is for the simple-minded. I am of the opinion that it was appropriate to expect something better. But let's not be discouraged. Our communities are young and they have a long way to go. In another 70 or 80 years they will have achieved international glory in science, letters, politics, art, and finance. Amerigo Ruggiero.[52]

In his letter to the readers of *La Settimana*, Ruggiero only reconfirms what he had argued in his chapter on the second generation: "Italian immigration to the United States cannot exactly be called a success. At least up to now." In other words, no real personality of undisputed superiority has, in his opinion, yet to emerge from the ranks of the Italian Americans. However, he does point out that this stands to reason, given that the majority of immigrants are "made up of the poorest, the most backwards, most physically weak and least intellectually developed" and, consequently, ill-suited to face the difficulties of modern life.

The justification for such a claim is based on the conviction that the immigrants "could not bring to the new land a culture that they

52   Amerigo Ruggiero, *La Settimana* (21 February 1937): 2.

did not possess." Moreover, Ruggiero notes that the Italian American communities "have inconsistencies and defects dating back to our origins that cannot be remedied"; therefore, it is out of the question to have any great illusions, with the most dangerous being "those of individuals who come to America unaware of the particular composition of our group of immigrants and who expect to deal with them as a uniform and compact mass that just left Italian shores."

In order not to find oneself puzzled and speechless in front of an Italian who may seem "a new zoological species that no one had ever heard of," Ruggiero maintains that one must study objectively "what possibilities these new communities still offer from a national perspective and what is the best way for us not to miss the advantages and the capacity for development that this perspective offers." He warns that it would be absurd to pretend to preserve as Italian an entire mass of immigrants, since each year the Italian communities become less Italian. According to Ruggiero, the most damaging blow dealt to the *Italianità* of the Italian communities "was the law that closed immigration almost completely and the subsequent measures that made the closure inevitable."

PREFACE

Only Amerigo Ruggiero could write this long-awaited book. Like few others he knows America and our communities. Like no other he has followed the events of our transoceanic emigration and has studied its problems in their infinite variety of political, economic, moral, and social characteristics. And like no other he loves those brothers of ours who have struggled long and hard to earn their little place in the sun.

What is particularly captivating in the writings of this great journalist, who is also a talented writer, is the passion that enlivens both his books and articles without prejudicing the truth, thus proving that you can love and understand at the same time. There is no phenomenon concerning our transoceanic emigration that escapes his attentive eye and no part of the life of our communities that does not command his thorough and exhaustive investigation. He never indulges in any type of prejudice nor does he seek to deform or even veil the truth.

His analysis is often uncompromising and his descriptions are full of shadows that light is unable to disperse. And yet, there is not one page that arouses in the reader any feeling of annoyance or pain because there is always the certainty of finding ourselves in the company of a writer who is known for his extreme honesty. He is a true Italian, who is the first to suffer what cannot be kept quiet but who does not fear the truth, which is always welcome, and because he knows that on the final balance sheet virtues compensate for the wear and tear of errors and disparities.

And what virtues! I do not intend to summarize or even review this splendid book, which is about politics, sociology, art, and poetry. I wish, instead, to highlight a characteristic that makes it extremely interesting and valuable. I do not think I am wrong when I state that Ruggiero's book succeeds, against all intentions of its author, in presenting an ideal history of our country, or better yet of our people, from the Unification to the present day. Let me explain. In the aftermath of the Unification, the populations of southern Italy, which gave their maximum contribution to immigration, remained suppressed by the ancient feudalistic customs and by the new political system, from which they gained no benefit, whose mentality and traditional forms of private and social life were so foreign. And yet, those populations preserved in themselves such an amount of energy, virtue, talent, and resistance that radiated in the countries across the ocean where, among innumerable hardships, they rebuilt their lives. The act itself of emigrating, challenging the unexpected and the unknown, was already decisive proof of physical and moral vitality. A vitality that did not take long in affirming itself in the immense American world.

In the pages that follow, readers will see the quantity and the magnitude of the hardships that our fellow countrymen faced as they sought fortune in those distant lands: hardships of all kinds that had their origins in the widespread prejudices against the Italians in America, in the deficiencies of our communities, and (and this may seem incredible) in their own virtues, so decidedly different from the way of thinking and living of the environment that received them.

The sufferings and the multiple sacrifices in those years were unspeakable. The courageous who sought work across the ocean were spared no humiliation. Ruggiero's recollection of these experiences is astounding because you can sense that it is real and it breaks your heart. Our vision is often blurred before certain pages of grief and truth. And a question spontaneously rises from the heart: but how were these brothers of ours, these contemporaries of our fathers, able to resist, how were they able to tolerate so much adversity? And to know that today things have changed is not enough to console us.

It was precisely the native virtue of race that challenged all obstacles and subjected our immigrants to the scrutiny and judgment of the American world. Believed to be physically weak, they proved themselves to be tougher than the others: the Irish, the Polish, the Germans, the so-called "titans" of the North. Distrusted and under suspicion due to the myths surrounding the peasants of southern Italy, they proved themselves to be unparalleled in their respect for their duties, punctual on the job, and worthy of all trust. Judged to be examples of a degenerate race due to centuries-old misrule and sufferings, they astonished everyone by their restraint (they were, among other things, the only ones who did not get drunk), by their loyalty to any type of obligation, and by their relentless ability to sacrifice. The fact that they ended up being preferred to all others says it all. The American capitalists, the great entrepreneurs, sought out Italian manpower for its trustworthiness and for its high performance. It was a great victory. However, it was a victory that was to cause another war in the daily and ruthless competition among immigrant laborers from all over the world as well as the local labor force. How the Italians defended themselves and how they once again emerged victorious is recounted by our author in truly unforgettable pages.

One need only mention here that they were able to prevail because, having been left to their own devices in total solitude, they made a supreme appeal to their incomparable virtues that in the Fatherland had been restrained by an unkind political and social constitution. Ruggiero's investigation of this subject is of great interest and of extraordinary value for its understanding of our own domestic history. Ruggiero shows us that those compatriots of ours, who came from the most modest classes, demonstrated much greater abilities than those of the pompous bourgeoisie who, in the immediate aftermath of the political events, perpetuated the class oppression in southern Italy during the years of the Bourbon dynasty. Ruggiero shows us that the so-called *cafoni* humiliate, by comparison, the so-called *galantuomini*. He shows us that while the first succeeded in living off their labor, buy a home, and accumulate savings, the latter were thrown by the wayside like worthless pieces of junk. Ruggieri shows us (here the author's psychology is transformed into poetry) that, in the end, it was the *cafoni* who saved the *galantuomini*, those good-for-nothings without skills or personal resources who were able to live off the generosity of those principled laborers and whom they did not spare (even in America) every kind of deceit and fraud.

I would like, in this regard, to bring to the readers' attention a thought that spontaneously came to mind as I was reading these pages and which Ruggiero, moreover, only hints at without making it a point of explicit commentary. In other words, I would like to point out in this splendid affirmation of the *cafoni* over the *galantuomini* proof of the need, justice, and historical importance of the fascist revolution. It was this revolution's demolishing of the old legal system and squashing of the parasitic classes that created in southern Italy the suitable conditions for the formation of those middle classes that draw from work their political and economic dignity. Such is to say that our emigration across the ocean has, as it were, anticipated that selection of values and of classes that in the Fatherland could only have taken place in the years following the march on Rome. A most persuasive proof of this is that the liberalism of the old regime ended up being, in final analysis, a very serious obstacle to the free exercise, both economically and socially, of the sound forces and genuine energies of our people.

The same process that one sees each day in Italy by virtue of fascism can be observed in America by following, with the guidance of our author, the events and history of our communities. And all this because in America, like in Italy after the advent of fascism, the spontaneous forces of our people were able to operate in full freedom. Even over there like here the different regional differences have disappeared and national unity has imposed itself like a necessity of life that restored a fact of conscience. Even there like here one has heard that national solidarity is not only a moral precept but also the foundation that bestows on the individual the privileged title of nobility. Even there like here the new generation has replaced, mutatis mutandis, the old.

It is at this point that Ruggiero's book reaches great depth. What is the real situation of the children of our first immigrants, those who are called Italo-Americans? The canvas has its light and its sad shades. Even in America a new generation has emerged, physically attractive, mentally alert, the pride of their fathers, who after many years of labor and sacrifice often achieved substantial fortunes and have established themselves in all fields of production, including agriculture, industry, and commerce. A new generation that has nothing to envy from the native inhabitants with whom they measure up favorably in school and in all kinds of sports. However, one should not think that American society opens its doors wide to this new generation. Ruggiero explains this phenomenon very effectively. It is not a question of ostracism or ill will. One cannot even say that it is a question of recurring prejudices. The phenomenon is more extensive and involuntary and is a part of the great process of American assimilation that must be measured in historical cycles. But it is certain that the Italo-Americans' time will come and it will come soon. And they will overcome the last obstacles in a society used to forging ahead. We look at this Italo-American youth with profound emotion because under the strong pressure of ancestral subconscious remembrances, it represents ever more vigorously our race in the great America, the new Fatherland, and it will redeem, even in the dominion of the spirit, the first, heroic, and misunderstood Italian immigration.

Piero Parini
Rome, 28 October 1936 – XV – Year I of the Empire

INTRODUCTION BY THE AUTHOR

The book that we present to our readers is not one of statistics let alone a detailed history of our immigration to the United States. For those who would like to know specific facts and precise information and statistics about this phenomenon, we can only suggest comprehensive studies which, unfortunately, have been largely produced by American authors. As one can imagine, these works betray, some more than others, a prejudice against our people. Even if the statistics were exact (and oftentimes they are not) their interpretation is marked by misunderstanding and deception. There have only recently appeared some capable studies by Italo-American scholars who attempt to set the record straight. And lately there have also been some studies on migration questions published in Italian.

Our intention in this present work is to offer a panorama of the Italian immigration to North America, the transformations that our mass migration experienced in being transplanted in a foreign land, and what its future prospects are. We have chosen to focus on the less known aspects of our migratory phenomenon, those that, in implicating the responsibility of an entire class and of the governments preceding fascism, had been constantly ignored and deliberately kept quiet. We understand how some burning truths will not be appreciated by many who belong to any one of the categories described in the book. But it was time to shed light on the deficiencies and injustices that have impeded the development of our communities abroad.

We wanted above all to be sincere and honest with ourselves, without diminishing, hiding, and spreading a thin gauze over infected wounds. Not everyone will agree with our assessment. However, even those who disagree will not be able to ignore the effort of having wanted to illustrate the various aspects of our migratory experience and present a map to orient us in the enormous mass of contradictory facts that such a phenomenon presents for examination.

Italians, strange as it is to say, have never seriously dealt with these streams of people who left to enrich foreign lands. They devoted themselves least of all when the flow of Italian blood reached its peak. In the years prior to the war, they regarded it with Olympic indifference. For the majority of our fellow countrymen, America was a place where a bunch of outcasts who, by some oddity of fate or environment, often succeeded in making a fortune. In general, the act of emigrating was considered to be a sign of a derelict and the immigrant was looked at with masked scorn even by an old working stiff or by a youngster who had no other likely hope but to latch on to any white-collar post whatsoever even for fifty lire a month. In Italy, interest in America began in the post war years when, with the famous exchange rate of one dollar to thirty lire, a number of sudden millionaires who had left their villages a few decades previously dirt poor flooded into the homeland. And this interest increased when it was seen that some people who had ventured to cross the ocean to explore cautiously the situation returned, after a six months stay, with their pockets full. It was a time of abundance, of that famous American prosperity: our good countrymen did not want their fellow villagers to return to the homeland disillusioned and thus filled their pockets with handfuls of dollars. At that time, dollars were a plenty and blow the expense! Unfortunately, immigration began to be studied seriously when it no longer existed. It was the fascist government that fueled the flame of *italianità* in our colonies as it was about to be extinguished, gathered together what had remained from the disorganization of the preceding years, and began to remedy the sad legacy of past governments.

The readers of this book will become aware of many things that those who reside in Italy are hardly able to appreciate. They will understand how, given the original constitution of our communities, these immigrants have very little or no influence on American life. Our readers will learn how, as a result of the partial or total illiteracy of our immigrants, all cultural initiatives had to be abandoned and those who had organized them returned to Italy discouraged and disillusioned. Furthermore, they will learn why there was never a successful circulation of Italian books and newspapers among our American colonies. How Italian theatrical companies of all types, after triumphant tours in South America, would arrive in New York where they expected to find even greater success, only to be forced to disband following disastrous results. How famous artists performed in front of empty seats and how actual collections were organized to send back to the homeland brilliant speakers who had come to bowl over America. However, this did not stop them from announcing that they had achieved astounding triumphs. And that is the worst lesson of the entire state of things. Very few are honest enough to report what they actually saw and what they really encountered during their American experiences. The misconception continues and others are encouraged to repeat the same fiasco. It is useless to try to stimulate culture if our old immigrant communities simply do not have any culture. If they read books, they are along the lines of *Reali di Francia* [The Royal House of France], and if they go to the theater, it is to see works like *Iena del Cimitero* [The Hyena of the Cemetery] or *Mafiusi della Vicaria* [Heroes of the Penitentiary].[1] The cultural lever can be activated among the new generations of Italo-Americans or among the youngsters who came here after the war. For the large majority of the Italian ex-patriots, they should aim for the results obtained by the Japanese in California. None of the little "yellow" men appear on lists of American charitable relief because the Japanese communities take care of their poor and unemployed. They have their own schools in which instruction for children born in America is delivered in the Japanese language. Moreover, they have established an organization that assists them in difficult circumstances, guides them so that they do not get into any trouble, defends them in the event they enter into conflict with people of other races or run into the hard measures of the American penal code. In all sincerity, let's admit that the comparison cannot be fully sustained. If anything, it is merely a question of numbers: the Italians are approximately five million while the Japanese do not exceed 150,000. However, if, at least in the more important communities, there were coordinated efforts to approach such a goal, any energy or money spent in this regard would be repaid by the consideration and respect that Italians on American soil have not as yet enjoyed. It would be most satisfying if this study succeeds in proposing a portrait of our colonies in the United States as they really are and not how they are depicted in the imagination of those who, not being familiar with them, invent, in order to suit themselves, enchanted castles that fall apart upon first contact with reality.

The Author

---

1   See footnotes 26, 27, and 28 in the Introduction to the Translation of this study.

I. THE LAST ARRIVALS

When the tide of immigration to the United States began to intensify and take a sharp turn in the year 1880, the American republic was organizing and strengthening itself into that state of widespread prosperity and well-being soon to be known the world over. The open wounds from five years of civil war were in large part healed, the ruins and destruction repaired, and the hatred between the North and South, which had been enflamed during the struggle and greatly intensified during the so-called *reconstruction* [in which the victorious operated in the States of secession as if they were in a conquered territory], began to fade into a healthy oblivion with the arrival of new generations. America benefited from the recent contribution of wealth coming to it from a South that had become definitively and concretely part of the Union. The days of the *frontier* were already a thing of the past. The chaotic, colorful, adventurous, and roguish period of assaulting ships, of unpunished crimes, of systemic violence had come to an end. But also ending was that period of the discovery of enormous wealth and the revelation of original, new, and fresh energies, along with a sharp and lively intelligence that rose to nurture them. It was a period that reached its peak with the *gold rush* in California and the unforgettable march toward the West: one of the most romantic transmigrations of people in modern times. After the destruction of the Indians and buffalo, the boundless lands of the Golden West were open to white colonization. Free land was for everyone. It was land offered to those who felt capable of farming it with intense love and unflinching toil: the secret, desperate aspiration of an infinite number of Europeans hailing from semi-feudal countries where every inch of soil available was monopolized by the large estate, that dead hand that immobilized any innovative activities and blocked any possibility of making money.

Free land to everyone had great consequences for the American nation. The circulation of wealth penetrated every level of society. The healthy sap trickled down to nurture the tenuous and outer roots. It was a glorious era for the economy of the United States, a new age in the history of mankind in which the fruits of progress and civilization could be enjoyed not only by a slim 10 per cent, as in the countries of the Old World, but by 80 or 85 per cent of the entire population. This is the only real great gift that America has given to humanity: the concept and practice of the enjoyment of tangible assets, education, health, beauty, and joys of the spirit on behalf of the largest number of people. This was a long way from the monstrous money grubbing organizations of financial *trusts* and monopolizing super industrialism that would transform a population of well-to-do and small landholders into a population of slaves who do not own anything: no roof, no bread and, even much less, the right to work and live. No one could have imagined then that 85 percent of the national wealth would end up in the hands of a privileged few who represent 5 percent of the population and that the unthinkable concentration of wealth would unleash a terrible economic crisis from which it is hard to see how the wealthiest nation in the world would be able to recover. But the benefits of the opening up of a virgin land with unlimited resources were not only material. There developed among Americans an abiding faith in their individual capabilities, in the institutions, in the political and social system of their country, and in the country's barely tapped boundless natural resources. One earned and one spent happily with the assurance that the sources of income would never end. From this belief there emerged an optimism that amazed the Europeans. What most pleasantly surprised them was that bonhomie and unaltered calm, that air of "good will," of evangelical benevolence. It was that natural impulse of wanting to be of assistance to everyone that prompted those who made money to do their best to have those around them prosper.

The willful readiness to set friends and acquaintances on the right path *to make money* was one of the most pleasing characteristics of America in those years. One looks back now with nostalgia to that atmosphere of "good will" and to that inclination to extend a friendly hand to whoever was in need. One thinks back to that era as an idyllic period for humanity with the vain hope that it will return. No one envied the income of others nor the capabilities of others to obtain financial and career successes. Instead, they admired them and were motivated to emulate them. Whether it was a lot or a little, there was enough for everyone. Europeans could not comprehend the state of mind of a similar society. They came from countries where competition is extreme and where they commonly ripped a piece of bread out of each other's mouths, and where it was prudent to pretend to be poorer than one actually was in order not to attract serious resentment, to avert annoying requests, and to avoid being the target of tax authorities. The Europeans were left stunned at how Americans not only showed off their wealth but also encouraged others with booming laughter and a slap on the back. In Europe, it was almost a necessity, a defense mechanism, to become impoverished, wear worn clothing, appear pitiful, take pride in acting like a bum, and glorify one's indigence as if it were an honor. In America, one was easily prone to exaggeration and *bluffing*. Those who earned ten boasted that they earned twenty and spent for thirty, relying upon an increase in future earnings. They loved generosity, gaiety, smiling faces. They hated *meanness*, frugality, privation, an air of sadness and dissatisfaction. The cities, having emerged from their colonial shell, were expanded and beautified. The newly built homes, even those for the working class and for those of modest means, were equipped with bath tubs, central heating, hot water, and in more recent times electrical and gas hook ups for stoves. Additionally, there were a number of other amenities that, even in the most developed European countries, only the wealthiest would be able to acquire at enormous costs. Included in the cost of rent of the apartments, one already found built-in closets to store clothing, *ice boxes* to store food, garbage chutes, ceiling fans for the circulation of air and all types of provisions that were indispensable to the complex life of the American communities. With money being easy and secure, life assumed an air of refinement and carefreeness, especially among the upper classes who felt inclined to follow the model of European society with regard to elegance, entertainment, and culture. These were the years between 1890-1900 that, due to the carefreeness and joy of life that characterized it, were known as the *gay nineties*. Even the outward appearance of the people became more refined. At least in the cities and among the classes that began to elevate themselves above the primitive masses, there disappeared the roughness of manners and language that smacked of *pioneerism*, the awkwardness in dress, the lack of interest in anything that does not have to do with material interests. With one big swoop, large moustaches, imposing beards, ridiculous sideburns were swept away, and there appeared, shaved to perfection, the figure of the clean shaven American that the world has known for over fifty years. Women were changing even more rapidly than men and advancing toward the highly qualified type, both intellectually and aesthetically, of the modern American woman. The wide hips of the far off days of the *pioneers* and the *frontier* were trimmed down to produce proportionate and slender physiques. The fat cheeks, massive jaws, and the flat and pale peasant-like faces grew refined in the features of the *girls* of the new continent: thin, irritable, fickle, eager to the point of an obsession to see, explore, and learn all that is new, interesting, beautiful, and horrible in the world. Slowly but surely, they broke the fetters of the Victorian age, assisted more than obstructed by their men. From the dawn of history, women enjoyed great respect among the communities that, to put it quite simply, we shall call Anglo-Saxon and among people of the North in general. The bitter struggle against a closed, cruel, and hostile nature could not afford to do without the work of half of the human race keeping it confined to restricted areas of the house. In their ancient European habitat, the northern woman stood alongside man in the relentless war against the atmosphere of implacable harshness. Once transplanted in the New World, she helped him cut the primitive forest, cultivate the corn, and fight against the Indians. Equality of duties leads to equality of rights, and woman's place in America was never one of subjugation and humiliation. No sooner had the American man shored up his acquisitions in order to give himself a pause, he apportioned a good part of his earnings for the intellectual and physical development of the feminine side of his own family. The woman was not slow to take advantage of it. She improved her personal hygiene, refined her dress, and enriched her diet, which had remained very simple and unvarying from the days when the main worry was to put a roof over one's head and secure a raw meal. Subsequently, she threw herself full force into any kind of social activity. She threw herself heart and soul into a career in the arts, sciences, industry, and commerce. She also devoted herself enthusiastically to sports where she became most adept. In order to complete this brief overview of American society during the peak years of our immigration to the new continent, it is necessary to remember how our immigrant communities bear the imprint that the Anglo-Saxons had impressed upon them. No matter how you want to judge this type of civilization, it was uniform and served to establish a certain rule in the communities comprised of people who descended from the four corners of the world. Despite its limited horizons and being insular, self-righteous, hypocritical, saturated in medieval prejudices as well as unjustified and persecuting hatreds against all that did not conform to it, the Anglo-Saxon civilization executed, until the world war, the important function of representing an order, if not *the* order, of providing moral and civic *standards*. *Standards* of this type were not lacking in the heterogeneous masses assembled here. They were, however, divided by their historical origins and by their objectives and they contrasted harshly in their essence. The dams had not yet burst and nor had there turned up suddenly the horrendous moral chaos of the post war years. The last years of the Victorian age in America also displayed an attractive poetic, romantic, and sentimental side before there burst onto the scene the disorganized and tumultuous period of *Americanism*. Those years were suffused with a certain peace, a certain tranquility of things that were dying, of *mellowness*, the calm and golden sweetness of October sunsets, of fruit that ripens on the branches, of deep autumn days when the reddish brown leaves gather with their slow rustling at the foot of an old, ivy-covered building.

* * *

In a society that had reached a certain equilibrium, albeit temporary, there poured in the great waves of our immigration. This will help to explain many things and, above all, the hostility with which it was greeted. From its beginnings, there had always been immigration to America. However, a large part of the immigration prior to 1880 consisted of northern peoples whose customs, temperament, ideas, and also physical appearance were more akin to the Anglo-Saxons. It is not that some groups of the northern immigration did not, in time, raise serious concerns. When the semi-savage masses of Ireland flooded into the United States like a restless torrent, they had not gone beyond, in their own country, a tribal stage. Midway through the last century, following the failed crop of potatoes, which constituted the principal, if not the only, food of the population, a devastating famine struck like a scourge on the island. Ireland unleashed on the United States the entire surplus of its famished, its crippled, its dim-witted, its deranged, its criminals and people, in general, whose experiences and ideas did not exceed the boundaries of a *clan*. The Irish immigrants always had their behavior shaped by the narrow customs and ferocious commandments of the new *clans* that were established on American soil. They are the ones who keep the police courts busy today and contribute enormously to *bread lines*, sanatoriums, and homeless shelters. Having worked their way into American politics where they brought with them the mentality, practices and dominant system of the *clan*, they became the main cause of the terrible corruption that infects it. They came in millions. And the tide reached its peak in 1851. From all parts a call to arms was heard. One feared their ignorance, aggressive brutality, popery, fanaticism, religious bigotry, a predisposition toward alcoholism and toward a chronic and shameless laziness. The arrival of the Germans, which amassed imposing proportions almost in the same period after the strikes in the textile industries of Silesia and following the political uprisings of 1848, sparked profound animosities and gave rise to rulings that were anything but favorable. Considered *desirable* by the racist propaganda of recent years due to similar blood lines with Anglo-Saxons, German immigration had previously been judged quite severely by Benjamin Franklin. With regard to the German immigrants, he states: "Those who come hither are generally of the most ignorant Stupid Sort of their own Nation [...] Not being used to Liberty, they know not how to make a modest use of it." However, when the Italians began to arrive in considerable numbers in the United States, the immigration of northern countries gradually diminished, and in some cases, such as that of the Germans, which, in the twenty-five years that preceded the world war, dropped to insignificant proportions as a result of the great industrial development that had occurred in Germany. From an ethnic as well as a social and economic point of view, the American republic had reached a relatively stable system. The northern immigration had been, if not completely assimilated, on its way to assimilation. In any case, it did not raise any serious concerns and no longer constituted a problem, with the exception, as mentioned, of the Irish who introduced into American life a permanent element of imbalance. The first leap forward was made by the Italians in 1880 with more than 12,000 new arrivals. In 1888, the number climbed to 51,000. From then on, the increase was constant with an occasional brief decline in the years of the American economic crises. 100,000 came in 1890 and increased to 285,000 in 1907. It reached its ceiling of 296,000 in 1914. Not being a scientific study, the numbers above have been rounded off. The first groups of immigrants came from the northern regions of Italy. Those populations were generally used to trading with foreign countries and facing risks and hardships in distant lands. They also benefited from more serviceable roads in relation to the almost inaccessible South and from its proximity to the great maritime outlet of Genoa. However, with the industrial and agricultural development in the North, those streams began to decrease dramatically, only to be rapidly overwhelmed in numbers by the floods of exiles who abandoned the southern shores. Since it was the immigrants of southern Italy who bestowed their special character on the entire Italian migration to North America—in their tragic, ridiculous, shameful, colorful, praiseworthy or reprehensible characteristics—our study will focus almost exclusively on them.

* * *

During the period in which the migratory movement gained its impetus, the South had reached the extreme limit of its resources. National unity did not bring with it the advantages that the people of the South had hoped. The Bourbons provided no schools, roads, aqueducts, drainage systems, railways, and no sanitary and hygienic measures. It was a corrupt and uncivilized government. However, under the Bourbon rule, the taxes were few and tolerable. With the unification of Italy, the South received a very small amount of the wonderful things that had been promised and had to pay for them with a very heavy tax disproportion that left much of its population on its knees. In other words, the South had to contribute with its taxes to the development of other regions of the peninsula, leaving its people empty-handed watching others as they filled their pockets. The large sacks crammed full with slabs of silver and gold coins resting at the bottom of the trunks of the well-to-do families, middle classes and prosperous farmers began to shrink rapidly. The southern regions plunged into an abyss of misery and remained more than ever in the conditions of a Balkan state out of which it could be dragged only by the advent of fascism. Besides the disproportionate tax pressures, another extremely important cause was added to produce the economic damage of the ancient Kingdom of Two Sicilies. Up until 1860, the South was heavily wooded and the breeding of ovine and bovine livestock represented one of the main sources of wealth. Having carried out the deforestation upon the enticement of more profitable farming methods, such as that of wheat farming on hillside lands, there occurred what always happens in these cases. The few years of abundant crops that the virgin soil produced are followed by entire decades of shortage and real famine. The practice of integrated soil fertility and of working the land so that the richest and tillable layer does not slide into the valley was still unknown. There suddenly appeared the problems of water runoff and the disruption of climate in the region. The fields became barren, arid, and infertile. Malaria extended its reach and wreaked havoc. The poverty and the complete abandonment of those populations by the ruling classes fostered the spread of all the antisocial phenomena that accompany the extreme ranks of poverty: oppression, exploitation, ignorance, superstition, unorganized insurrections, and crime. The social strata that most suffered these conditions call to mind, even in their external forms, past eras and biblical disasters. They are the most oppressed and without hope for redemption who find within themselves the energy to move forward and abandon a land that appeared to reserve for them only struggles, rags, and diseases. Day laborers, share-croppers and, subsequently, the lowest representatives of a primitive artisanal trade were the first to set out. And it took a great deal of strength for these people who knew only their tiny village square and the shape of their own bell tower. They abandoned their native land, separated themselves from their loved ones, and ventured into an immense unknown country in which language and customs were ignored and, to arrive there, it took fifteen or twenty days on the boundless ocean. We will make a statement that may stun some intransigent supporters of the superiority of the Nordic people if they happen to see it. It took more energy, more moral strength, more initiative, and more fighting spirit and a sense of adventure on the part of the southern immigrants who came to settle on American soil than it did on their northern predecessors upon which so much value is placed in the United States. It is because the latter had a virgin continent before them where, in the absence of any rivalries and competition, they were able to settle in their own way, continue to speak their own language, observe their own religion, and establish under another sky their own laws, customs, and traditions. Real hardships were many and severe. This is so true. And the dangers were also many. However, at the end of the day, nothing more was required of them but excessive physical exertion and doing away with some Indians. With Bible in hand and after obtaining from these unfortunate *savages* all the help and information necessary to withstand the hard times, the good Anglo-Saxons dedicated themselves with great fervor to their elimination. Such was the case each time they would secure a new stretch of land and extend their occupation into unknown territories. Instead, for our people the undertaking was much more desperate: they had to confront hostile populations who had already settled for some time in the country and who did not spare these new arrivals any humiliation or harshness. They had to learn as best they could a difficult language that was very different from their own; they had to adapt to new and strange customs; and they had to assume a different mentality and new sensibilities. Furthermore, after a series of internal commotions and suppressed rebellions, they were seemingly hardened as a result of hearing at every step all that is held most dear insulted and laughed at. They had to surrender any sense of pride and self-respect and make it on their own without any help or means—not even the indispensable tools of the alphabet and the basic notions of hygiene and good manners—amongst people who are deeply rooted in their land who throw in your face their vulgar and fat opulence that crushes you before you move. They are unable to protest against brutal regimes because they did not know the language. In brief, this is what our immigrants had to deal with on American soil. Despite the tremendous obstacles before them and despite their state of inferiority in the initial struggle, they managed to come out triumphant in tenacious and uncompromising competitions against groups who were considered by right of birth to have total command of the country: political, social, and economic.

Many years of malnutrition, malaria, and isolation did not certainly make our immigrant classes an able-bodied race with a powerful body and attractive qualities. They were skinny and gaunt with bent and shrunken bodies. They had a dragging gait and dangling arms. They had no concerns about keeping themselves or their clothing clean. They had dark and heavily furrowed faces, shaggy, matted hair, tattered and unkempt clothes. The last straw was that these men insisted on wearing a large, dark moustache in a country where, for quite some time, a real aversion had developed against facial hair. Faces had to be smooth and shiny like the palm of one's hand. They had always lived in fear: the oppression under which they had been held by the ruling classes, both the Bourbon governments as well as the so-called liberal government; the failed harvests; diseases; frequent deaths in the family; the daily struggle even to obtain a simple jug of water; the misfortunes and calamities of all kinds that showered on them like hail. The fear of all these things had bestowed upon them a look that was between frightened and surly, as if they suspected every new face to be an enemy and a hostile act by anyone who approached them. For Americans, it was the most glaring revelation of their wicked mind and devotion to evil. Because this is the way Americans reason. And the earrings! In some southern villages, it is common to pierce the ears of baby boys at birth in order to wear specially shaped little earrings. It was to protect them from the evil eye. However, this was not only a custom in Italy. Some maritime populations of other countries, such as Brittany, have the same custom. And in America, as far as I know, no one has ever dreamed of criticizing the French for this. If those in Italy could just imagine the harm that the large, black moustache and earrings have caused! On more than one occasion, some immigration official (we are talking about the period of unrestricted immigration) proposed to reject men wearing earrings under the pretense that they were *gypsies* or, at the very least, "Orientals." Even now, when a prize competition might be established for some old rare surviving wearer of earrings, in the music halls, motion pictures, and in the costume *parties* of high society, the stereotyped figure of the Italian is that of a kind of brigand-faced mulatto, with large hoops dangling from the ears, an enormous dark moustache and a head covered with a colored bandana knotted around the neck. A seventeenth century pirate! Americans do not easily change their ideas, especially when they grow fond of certain stereotypes. The one that is applied to us is the stereotypical image of the pirate. In a recent publication of a trip to Italy, two dimwitted American women candidly confess to not having seen one organ grinder with his ever-present monkey perched atop his music box. For them, this had to come as a huge surprise. Unfortunately, as we have noted above, this type of immigration arrived in the United States when our country had managed to transform itself and was making great strides toward advancement. It would have made a much less favorable impression a few decades ago during the mad scrambling aboard ships when everyone wore a moustache or a beard and no one cared about how they dressed and paid very little attention to cleanliness and personal appearance. Even more unfortunate was the fact that the hordes who came from our southern regions chose not to head toward the countryside, where their presence would not have aroused much attention; instead, they clustered in the heart of the city's neighborhoods, in the same dwellings where the Irish had previously lived. These latter were quick to clear out, prompted by this powerful migratory wave that was fresh off the boat from Europe. The conflicts between the Irish and the Italians were frequent and bloody. The Irish were instigators and bullies who were enlivened by a religious fanaticism that made them view the new arrivals as jailers of the Pope. The Italians, on the other hand, were hostile and resentful. The clash between these two ethnic groups caused many deaths. It is only in recent years that they have appeared to reach a *modus vivendi* of mutual tolerance.

The impression that the Americans had of these strange, small, dark individuals, who were continually excitable and vociferous, was a mixture of curiosity, dismay, and disgust. The habits that our immigrants uprooted and brought with them from their villages of

Sicily, Calabria, Abruzzi, and Lucania to the heart of populated cities, which were on the verge of becoming large metropolitan centers, were certainly not made to be modified. The women were seated on the steps of their houses calmly attending both to their own and to their children's intimate hygiene. This included checking the children's hair for lice and breast-feeding them in full view of everyone in a country that considers such an activity "shocking." Other women, who were in an advanced stage of pregnancy and with the front of their dresses raised several inches above the ground, crossed the most fashionable of the city's streets carrying on their heads bundles of wood they had gathered from buildings undergoing demolition. In America, such things could only be found in the most remote mountain regions inhabited by "poor whites." And then there was all the rest. In the middle of the cities, one observed processions honoring the saints of our small villages pass in front of mocking Americans. These occurred after the vain attempt of opposition by the local Catholic bishops against whom our enraged peasants were accused of threatening physical harm. Along with the processions, there were the bands, lighting sculptures, fireworks, and Italian nougat candy and hazelnut stands. In the middle of all this bedlam, the city streetcars, packed with people who laughed and shouted vulgarities and insults, slowly proceeded. And the routine death that was part of the normal balance sheet of the celebration. The Americans ended up getting used to such spectacles. But from then on there entered into their mind that feeling of aversion, be it tacit or pronounced, that found its concrete and definitive expression in the law against immigration.

II. NORTH AND SOUTH IN AMERICA

There was a reason for the concentration of our immigrants in the urban centers. Controlled from the moment of their landing by the so-called *bosses*—middlemen in the labor trade who conducted the twofold role of recruiters and exploiters—the poor immigrants were put to work immediately upon arrival. Ignorant of the language, customs, and labor system, they had no other choice. They worked the most humble and hardest jobs reserved for the "unskilled," for those who had no specialized trade: generally jobs digging foundations and carrying the supplies necessary for the opening of roads and tunnels, to the construction of buildings and railroads. It was employment that did not require any waiting nor training and not even the knowledge of one word of English. It was hard work and often dangerous: dangers increased by the negligence of companies to apply the necessary measures to protect the life of an anonymous herd of foreigners for whom no one cared. Countless Italian laborers lost their lives, crushed by falling concrete and collapsing earth at the construction sites of the *subways* and *skyscrapers*, suffocated in sewers, dismembered by dynamite and gas line explosions, and rendered shapeless by the railways and by an infinite number of other catastrophes that could have easily been avoided with a little more forethought and spending.

The hard labor was aggravated by the brutality of the *bosses*, who were almost always Irish and who employed the same methods to the team of workers under their supervision to those prevalent in the South for the black chain gangs in the cotton fields. The tyrant was always there ready to implore, incite, urge, abuse, yell, curse, and fire on the spot anyone who lingered to take a breath, exchange a word with a companion or did not achieve a level of productivity that, according to the calculations of standardized cost-effectiveness, one could expect from the human machine driven to its maximum forced speed. In the most remote regions outside the protection of civilization, these *bosses* were real criminals who, besides committing every type of theft, aggression, and abuse, were used to suppressing any sign of discontent and rebellion with gun shots. The dead body was made to disappear quickly and the matter was closed. Especially in the early years of immigration, many of our workers who appeared to have been swallowed up by the earth as a result of their silence ended up being bumped off by tyrants enraged by the slightest sign of opposition or transformed into wild beasts by the alcoholism to which they had fallen prey. A word misunderstood, a bold gesture, the secret complaint of alleged machinations were enough to bump off a man with greater swiftness and indifference than what it took to kill a rabid dog. With that special sadistic cynicism of the Northerners, the supervising executioner, having completed the killing, calmly proceeded to add another notch on his gun, which he would every once in a while proudly show to his friends of the same ilk so that they would count how many *damned foreigners* he was able to silence forever. The man who could boast a very large number of notches enjoyed in the entire construction site, and among those forced to bend under his brutality, great respect as a man of courage and decisiveness. And it was not wise to joke around with him. The punishment for these matters was absolute. The tremendous power of the companies intervened time and again to protect the henchmen who guarded the employers' interests so that they emerged unscathed from any difficulty in which they might be entangled as a result of their savage acts.

In spite of the dangers and brutal treatment, our workers experienced great advantages from employment in America. For many of them, it felt like arriving in Paradise and resulted in an excessive attachment to their adopted country that one observed in returning immigrants. This infatuation induced a reaction on the part of their fellow Italians who found their boasting intolerable, their comparisons irritating, and their stories incredible. In the first place, the work day was eight hours. In the homeland, no one counted the working hours in the fields: the usual measure was from sunrise to sunset. And then, there was that new, extraordinary thing that made them face each sacrifice light-heartedly: a guaranteed, clear cut compensation in cash for their work at week's end, which was an unfulfilled and unattainable aspiration of their entire previous life. During their time spent in the homeland, in compensation for interminable days of wearying labor, they earned little money in addition to the meager meals that their masters deducted from their salary. Often the payment of a dozen copper coins was deferred, postponed endlessly, and completely vanished. They had worked for a paltry sustenance: always with their clothes torn, always caught up with repairing their shoes, the purchasing of a little oil and salt, and the rent payment for the shack where they lived. Their weekly salary in dollars made them subconsciously feel on a superior social level and they acquired a greater self-confidence and self-esteem. They began to lose the air of a beggar that they brought with them to the New World and that had been fostered by the foreigners' many unfair judgments, which were lacking in tolerance and humanity. The average pay for our immigrants was seven dollars a week. A fortune! They found a way to live on this money while being able to send three or four of these dollars to their family in Italy. How these immigrants were able to live on three or four dollars a week, and oftentimes even less, is one of the most painful and tragic, but at the same time heroic, chapters of our immigration to America. The low standard of living to which they subjected themselves shocked the Americans more than any other trait of this new population arriving from overseas. Not understanding its magnitude and not appreciating the beauty and sanctity of their sacrifice, the Americans saw in the inhuman conditions to which the Italian immigrants adapted their sad existence a sign of incurable degeneration, a threat to the economic *standard* that they had achieved, and a danger to the moral and physical health of the entire population. Our immigration, and the Mediterranean immigration in general, differed from that of the Nordic regions in one very essential feature: there was a shortage of women. It consisted largely of able-bodied men from 18 to 45 years old. While the Northerners, both in war and in transmigrations, were always accompanied and assisted by their women, the Mediterraneans preferred to keep them protected and watched over until they were able to reunite with them. The previous wave of immigrants either travelled with their women or had them come as soon as possible. They settled permanently in the country and the European chapter of their life came to an end. This earned them greater respectability and a sense of stability and economic superiority compared to our fellow countrymen who remained for an indefinite period, often quite long, as if they were suspended and aimless. However, the attachment to one's land, no matter how much pain it had caused, was very strong and not easily eradicated. They did not see America as a permanent residence but rather as a place where one came to make money, where one suffered terribly, and from where one fled as soon as a little money had been set aside. This sum, scraped together at the cost of inhuman sacrifices, was to go toward the purchase of a piece of land on which they would live the remainder of their days with their own families who were relieved from poverty. There they would build a new and comfortable little house that would become the envy of their neighbors and would identify them as *americani*. By and large, this long-harbored dream was crushed. After spending the money for the purchase of property or the construction of a home, they were completely drained, without any money to yield anything from that small piece of land whose modest size was also unable to assure them any existence. With a personal stoicism and great determination, they began the return journey only to start over the *via crucis* from the very beginning. It was not uncommon to repeat this experiment three, four, five times with the result being that their savings were eaten up by the shipping companies—many of which, alas, were foreign—before resigning themselves to saying a definitive good-bye to their homeland and bringing family and children to the new land. It was the most grievous indictment that the Americans advanced against our immigrants. They did not come, like those from the northern countries, to contribute to the prosperity and development of the nation. Indifferent to everything that took place around them, they remained an immutable and unassimilable mass that did not participate in the life of the country. They were only concerned about accumulating a certain amount of money, subjecting themselves to sacrifices that no civil human being would be capable of tolerating without remaining forever ruined in body and wounded and humiliated in one's human self-esteem.

To go and work the land was out of the question. Our peasant arrived in America terrorized by the many years of poverty and hard work spent on a thankless soil that spoiled the most tenacious efforts and rewarded the enormous labor devoted to cultivate it with a crop that was almost nil. His was a state of exasperation against any thing that had to do with the land and that reminded him of the old job whose only outcome was unknown disappointments and woes. He preferred to dedicate himself to any other unhealthy and humiliating work provided that he would see something in his hand at week's end and without having to wait an entire year in the hope, which very seldom occurred, of a little money to obtain the most indispensable consumer goods and to deal with basic needs. No matter how primitive his standard of life was, it still could not be reduced to the existence of a troglodyte. Ultimately, it was one of those hatreds of unrequited love. Deprived of their modest plot of land, the day laborer, the old tenant farmer, and the small farm owner hated the ground that rendered much less than the trust put in it and did not match the intense love that they had devoted to it. And proof that this was a temporary indignation is revealed by the fact that as soon as they were able to set aside a small sum—oftentimes much too small— they would rush, with a renewed faith and revived hopes, to try the experiment in their homeland again. Misguided and distracted by mixed feelings in the early days, they did not benefit from any of the marvelous opportunities that the new country offered in order to take root in its soil and lead a more independent and respectable life. The abundance of lands available was nearly unlimited and could be obtained for almost nothing. The biggest difficulty was the lack of money necessary to enhance their value. Let us say straight away that the difficulty would not have appeared overwhelming if our immigrant had been endowed with a resourcefulness and the necessary resolve to penetrate into the forests, chop the trees, build a cabin from their trunks, conduct drainage works, grow a corn field, hunt squirrels, turkeys, and wild rabbits, and set traps for animals with pelts. In short, they had to remain in the conditions of a modern Robinson Crusoe, as self-sufficient as possible. The rest would have come later and the reward for the work would have been adequate and, not infrequently, considerable. In other words, he would have had to be a *pioneer*, instead of a bootblack, navvy, or a street sweeper. But the Italian is not the *pioneer* type. He has been detached from nature too long to be able to love it and to feel an integral part of it. The urbanization of Italy began from Roman times. The depopulation of the countryside was a result of the creation of world villages where the agrarian population lived concentrated around these developments after the work in the fields, which remained something outside and detached from ordinary life. The Middle Ages only aggravated this condition and, unfortunately, the Middle Ages, for the South, lasted until the advent of fascism. The threat of deadly malaria did not allow them to sleep overnight in the fields and the general security of the village was even more precarious. Since time immemorial, the peasants of the South have been used to walking many miles on foot with tools on their backs as they head to work and do the same on their return, tired as they are after a long day of toil. Malaria and brigandage accentuated, almost to the point of making it second nature, the tendency to stay very close, to group together, and sustain each other shoulder to shoulder. They need to see each other in the square, tavern, and coffee house in order to exchange a few words, sit at their doorsteps with neighbors in the evening, and gather together in their joys and sufferings. This tendency toward sociability, the result of a long-standing civilization, is one of the most likeable aspects of their character that foreigners never cease to praise and admire. However, it also has its drawbacks. The long-established urbanization has caused the Italian not to love and appreciate nature. He hates solitude which frightens and depresses him. He is not particularly fond of animals and plants, nor does he care for creeks and forests. He perceives natural things as vaguely hostile and incomprehensible. Capable of gushing over Bernini's colonnade or a Renaissance façade, he would hardly have been enthused by colonnades of gigantic trees that nature provides in the virgin forest or by the tumultuous passage of herds of bison, and rarely did he gaze in admiration at the perfect architecture with which a beaver builds his lodge. His first impulse was to destroy all this and replace it with stone. The senseless and criminal deforestation in the homeland as well as the almost absolute destruction of animal life that transformed the fields of certain regions of Italy into deserts is reflected in our literature which, from this perspective, is simply arid. This has been noted by foreigners who have harshly criticized the spiritual color blindness that distinguishes it. The return to the fields and the ruralization of Italy have recently become the cornerstones of the fascist program and are considered major reclamation projects of the regime. But we must not deceive ourselves. In order to root out old habits and replace them with a new *forma mentis* that, in the interest of the country, will lead to a respect for living things, plants and animals, much time and dedicated work will be necessary. It is natural that, given these tendencies, the Italian could not transform himself into a *pioneer*. In America, he did not participate in the ambitious and systematic endeavors of colonization like those accomplished by the Germans in Wisconsin and the Swedes in Minnesota. Apart from small collective farms that were set up in some states (Arkansas, Texas, Alabama) where several Italian agricultural communities were able to establish themselves with a certain success, our immigration remained largely urban. An exception needs to be made for the agricultural organizations of fruit and wine in California, but these are capitalist in nature. The other Italians who settled in the open fields did it individually after years in the city, which made it possible for them to accumulate the initial capital. They settled in sizeable numbers on farms in the Eastern states: Connecticut, New Jersey, and Pennsylvania. They were farms that the Americans had abandoned because of their meager yield and moved on to cultivate richer and virgin lands.

* * *

The need to remain united and to find themselves in an environment similar to the one they had abandoned resulted in our immigrants leading a life in their adopted land that followed the model of their little village where they were born and raised. They felt like aliens not only to Americans and all that was American but also to their fellow Italians. In America, it became especially evident that, despite the Unification, Italians felt anything but part of the same country. There were Sicilians, Calabrians, Abruzzesi, Pugliesi, but there were no Italians. Not even could one speak of regionalism; rather, a more strict, cautious, and surly *campanilismo* against others born under the spire of a different bell tower, even though it may be just a few miles from one's own. This phenomenon is explainable if not justifiable. The liberal governments were simply not prepared to proceed toward an actual unification of the nation. The immigrants did not have a common language. They had their dialects. They did not understand one another. To someone from Campania, the dialect of Abruzzi was strange and annoying, while others from different regions were unable to tolerate the Sicilian dialect. Every immigrant loved to hear the familiar sound of one's own native dialect ringing in one's ears and to be surrounded by the usual forms of life. They gathered, therefore, according to the region they came from, drawn to each other to the point of forming a chain. Entire neighborhoods were made up of people who came from just one region. In some streets there gathered by preference immigrants from a certain town who lived their same old ways: exchanging services, going and coming from their neighbors' homes, celebrating the patron saint's religious feast, establish fraternal societies named after a saint or a miraculous Madonna, organizing banquets and festivities for births and weddings according to the customs of the village. Enclosed in their own shell, they spend their days in the most absolute and blissful ignorance of the unknown world that surrounds them. If there was an incomprehension and lack of harmony and affinity among the Italians of different regions of the South, there existed a total abyss between the Italians of the North and those of the South. There would not have been a clearer and more profound division had they belonged to foreign countries. Northern immigration was of a completely different type than that of the South. For the most part, the workers from central and northern Italy went to America with a job. They were mosaicists, stone cutters, miners, gardeners, milliners, printmakers, weavers, wood carvers, and mechanics. In other words, they were specialized in various branches of production and industry. Contrary to the Sicilian sulphur miner, the lumberjack from the Sila, or the shepherds from Lucania, the Northerners came from urban centers. They knew what the needs of industrial communities were, what specific adjustments and limitations they required, and the implicit demands that one is subject to in order to coexist. They were inclined toward fellowship and mutual solidarity, which were indispensable if one were to emerge from the bitter labor struggles and the rough world of capitalist productivity with the least amount of damage possible. All this was new and incomprehensible to the Southerners who had lived in the rough and primitive individualism of the woods and unpopulated lands. Finding themselves suddenly right in the middle of industrial centers at the peak of production where an entire process of adjustment was necessary in order to survive without irritating and offending others in thousands of inconceivable ways, the Southerners looked like savages. As a consequence of the technical expertise obtained in their home country, the northern workers, having overcome the language difficulties, found employment rather quickly in the category of *skilled* laborers. This meant high salaries and job security. Moreover, they did not delay joining trade unions, putting themselves on par with American workers who held them in relatively high regard if only for this fact. One cannot even imagine how much the southern immigrants' longstanding reluctance and resistance to join the workers' organizations damaged them. Nor, in all fairness, can one fault them. Just like the modern Russians, they suddenly had to transform themselves from farmhands into factory workers. The psychology of being born and raised in an industrial center was completely foreign to them. They lacked the vision of the benefits that can be reaped from acting jointly for the common good and common defense. They did not understand the need to become part of organizations whose method of operation was beyond their practical experience and their capacity to detach themselves and formulate general ideas. They regretted having to pay the monthly contribution to the unions and saw it as a robbery to which they had to submit themselves. It was money taken away for no reason from the family budget. They considered the regulations and directives that the unions imposed in the interest of the working class as bizarre and tyrannical decrees for which they were unable to find a justification. The large American trade unions were quick to recognize this fact and sounded the alarm. They began a relentless campaign against this immigration that produced *scabs* or, as one used to call them in Italy, *crumiri*, who threatened with their unfair competition the standard of living of the American working classes. The attack was incessant and it continues today against every possible threat of importing foreign labor. The enormous pressure of labor organizations on government leaders must be considered as one of the principal causes of the stoppage of immigration to the United States.

The unequal ability to adapt to the new environment of the colonies of the North and those of the South was reflected in the contrasting standard of living. The difference of origin and place where they were raised and educated was displayed above all in their dwellings. The northern immigrants always had a better home, located in the so-called *residential* neighborhoods and inhabited by affluent people who guarded their tranquility and cleanliness and were ready to seek recourse against any infringement on the orderliness and peace of their community. The Northerners had no difficulty in assimilating with people of other races and were almost never cause for protests and complaints. Their houses were a model of cleanliness both outside and inside. They effortlessly remained updated to the necessary mechanisms and methods to maintain them. For the Southerner, unfortunately, it was an entirely different story. In the large cities, they adapted to the most despicable and shabby *slums* of the working-class neighborhoods. In small towns, the neighborhoods they inhabited were almost always located near gasometers and railroad stations where the very poor lived. They were often near the Black and Chinese neighborhoods, with all the degrading consequences that such close proximity generally produced. Nor, on the other hand, would it have been possible for the Southerners, especially in the early years of our immigration, to do differently even if they had the financial means. They were not welcome in the good neighborhoods. Even distinguished southern families often experienced the affront of being denied a small apartment by some filthy Irish custodian who exuded a stench of whiskey from her entire fat self as she repeated the stereotypical line: *we don't rent to Italians.* In some neighborhoods it was not even worth the trouble to inquire. There was a sign that informed you. Even if a landlord of a building were to overlook the prevailing prejudice and put an Italian family into one of his apartments, there would be the surprise of seeing all his other tenants leave. The best segment of the Southerners found themselves faced with certain hostilities and well-established opinions that drove them, in spite of their laudable efforts to escape, into the *slums* of the working-class neighborhoods. We said prejudice and prejudice it was insofar as they made no distinctions and placed everyone in the same category. But it wasn't so much prejudice because, to our dismay, it had some base of truth. Having come from our backwards villages, the rural population was simply not suited to living in confined quarters where every centimeter of space counts. The maintenance of the apartments in conditions of comfort, health and hygiene depends on a succession of operations rigorously established. Should one of these be missing, the regular development of family life is upset and proceeds haphazardly. Our peasants continued to live the same way in their new urban dwellings as they had lived in their small rustic homes where they came from. They neglected to clean the floors, which, being made of wood, were soon covered with a coat of grime that emitted throughout the home the stench of a chicken coop. The bathtub was used to place dirty laundry and trash. The toilets and water pipes frequently backed up due to the waste and foreign bodies with which, without thinking, they clogged them. One did not even think about washing the windows. This was essential in a country where factory dust and smoke dirtied them from one day to the other. Accustomed to do as they pleased without giving any thought to their neighbors, they followed the same pattern. In a working country where it is important to rest certain hours and where the home represents a haven of peace and quiet from the infernal chaos of the streets and factories, the pleasure of an hour of tranquility, of physical and spiritual abandonment after the tremendous tension of a day of hard labor, is dependent, in large part, on one's neighbors. One noisy neighbor ruins your life. Our immigrants did not understand any of this. They were restless into the late hours, would rumble up and down the stairs, shouting and yelling over nothing, while alarming the neighbors as if they were about to kill one another. They were visible at the windows and in the wide-open doorways, sloppy and undressed, causing scandal among some puritanical women who lived across the street and who hurried to slam the door in their face. On numerous occasions, fellow tenants or others from the neighborhood had to intervene and report to the "Society for the Prevention of Cruelty to Children" the physical abuse that parents used on their children. However one chooses to judge the matter, this is a country where children are allowed a great deal of freedom and severe physical punishment is a reminder of the Middle Ages. These immigrants became what in America is called a *nuisance*. Word quickly spread, and no one wanted them nearby. They were restricted to those types of ghettos called *Little Italy* where, unfortunately, they still live packed like sardines. This included those who could obtain much better lodgings. And so, the rural origin left its indelible mark. Even when he has become well-off, our peasant takes very little care of the home. It can be said that the major distinction of class that exists in the South is the home. The bourgeoisie always have a better home than the farm owners, although the latter live off the fat of the land while many *galantuomini* must buy bread in the square. The same philosophy has been transported to America. It is incredible how much is spent on food in a moderately wealthy Italian family. The waste of provisions is enormous. An American family would live a month on what an Italian family consumes in a week. Americans who participate in an Italian meal are left dumbfounded. The Italian tends to save on the home while the American, on the contrary, spends, at times, nearly half his earnings on the home. He will tighten his belt regarding food. Capable of getting by on a few cups of coffee and milk and two *sandwiches* a day, one has no idea how much an American can tighten his belt. The result, however, is that the American gives the impression of being much richer than the Italian because he lives in the best neighborhoods and in beautiful and expensive homes. The reality is entirely different: the American's life is precarious. He doesn't have a penny in his savings. A number of Italians who live in the *slums* can place under your nose bank books that will shock you. But their concept of life is not to increase the respect of our race on American soil. This would require less waste of money for superfluous food and more attention to personal appearance, not to mention decorum and cleanliness of the home. The Northerners did not want to be associated with this low esteem that the Americans held Italian immigration in general and they wanted to differentiate themselves. In doing so, they exaggerated and certainly did not contribute to the prestige of our country's name. Many ideas and current opinions, many of which have amounted to blatant defamation, that the Americans have of the Southerners were first spread by the northern Italians. Motivated by the preoccupation to distinguish themselves, they pinned on the Southerners a number of faults and bad qualities that in actuality they did not have. This desire to differentiate themselves got to the point that many Northerners, especially the Piedmontese from the textile industrial centers, preferred to pass themselves off as French. In these places, they gave the name *Vandea* to those neighborhoods inhabited by Southerners. It is not that there isn't a reason for even this deplorable lack of understanding. The first contacts between the two immigration groups were anything but felicitous, not to say disastrous. The Northerners' habits and customs were badly interpreted by the inhabitants of the South, especially concerning the freedom women enjoyed and the heavy consumption of alcohol. Having come from villages where there are rigorous mores and formalities even in the most humble of classes, they judged the freedom of action and the spontaneity of the Northerners to be *corruption*. The latter, in turn, found the Southerners' jealousy, testiness, air of suspicion or slight provocations to be intolerable. They considered them *brutes* with whom it was impossible to establish relations of peaceful and serene co-existence. The two were and remain divided still today. If by chance they come briefly into contact, they act like oil and water: they separate spontaneously. There are Northerner clubs where, either by tacit agreement or by the expressed prohibition of some article of rules, Southerners are not allowed. At first, such a phenomenon was cause of never-ending wonder and, later, even less consideration for the new immigrant element. What kind of people was this whose citizens, despite coming from the same country, did not understand each other? There occurred strange cases, which revealed a paradoxical and absurd status quo: a lost Italian boy who spoke no English was paired with another boy so that he could convey where he lived and anything else about himself: the two did not understand each other. One was Genovese, while the other was Neapolitan. At home they had only heard their respective dialects. Oh, those dialects! They have done us more harm than earthquakes and epidemics. I would like those people who in Italy still speak an Arcadian dialect and work for the preservation of dialects to take a trip to the countries of immigration. If among the immigrant masses it was not possible to spread and impart an

Italian culture to the new generations, it was because of the dialects. In the construction projects between Italian crews from one region and those from another, there would be, at times, fierce battles. The American *bosses* had to learn about the existing antipathies and animosities between the various groups to avoid their coming into contact with one another. This was the effect of sixty years of liberalism and an alleged democratic education: the spectacle of Italians being divided more than ever abroad has demonstrated how the unification of Italy, in its most important part, that of a communality of ideas and feelings among its citizens, was only a myth.

III. *CAFONI* AND *GALANTUOMINI*

In southern Italy, the farm workers who comprise the overwhelming majority of the population have been given the derogative name of *cafoni*. This term sums up all the coarseness, uncouthness, impenetrability, distrust, filthiness, superstition, and ignorance that for centuries have been considered attributes of the peasants. If such a term may not be entirely understood by an Italian from the North, when Southerners describe someone as a *cafone*, they know perfectly well what that means.

The country bourgeoisie is known collectively by the name *galantuomini*. For centuries, there has been an immense gulf between the *cafoni* and the *galantuomini*. They despise and scorn each other. The hatred and scorn are well-hidden in the *cafoni* under a thick layer of servility; instead, the *galantuomini* are overt, insolent, and devoid of human respect. The *cafone*, moreover, has an instinctive fear and an enduring distrust of the *galantuomo* with whom he tries to come into contact as little as possible. Due to a long and painful experience, he knows that any encounter with the *galantuomo*, any business transaction, any disparity concerning salaries, land boundaries, and trades have resulted, for him, in damages and injuries if not utter ruin. Taking advantage of his greater knowledge of the law and using his social position, connections, and contacts, the *galantuomo* has always been able to swindle the *cafone*. When the *galantuomo* could do nothing else, he would intimidate the *cafone*'s wife or daughter.

The southern bourgeoisie is a heterogeneous mixture that has been able to produce and prolong into modern times an overpowering, miserly, and shortsighted feudalism, along with a hasty emergence of Enlightenment ideas spread by the French revolution. On its branch of arrogant, disdainful *spagnolismo* from which a rigorous sense of a caste system pervades that flaunts its idleness as the most befitting quality of a well-born person, there are grafted ideas of equality and brotherhood that, inasmuch as they were whispered by university students, never captured the spirit of the class to which they belonged. At the time of triumphant socialism, the agitators complained that the sons of the southern bourgeoisie, even those who were most impassionate about the new ideas, returned to their homes after graduation and ended, once and for all, that period of folly, discarding it from their lives as if it never existed. They began to see things exactly like their fathers. In other words, it was a view that ended in the continued plundering of the plebs and in the continuation of a never-ending *status quo* of ignorance and oppression. Unfortunately, with regard to the South, one must talk about *plebe* and not the populace: *plebe* as in ancient Roman times, which has not changed from that period until the advent of fascism. In order for a community to earn the name of populace, there must exist a minimum common denominator of feelings, knowledge, and enjoyment of the benefits of life and culture in which the majority of its constituents partake. A millionaire and a laborer from the United States, who, not knowing one another, meet by chance on a train, at a party, or at a sporting event, would have a number of things of common interest to maintain a normal conversation: sports, the education of their children, who up to a certain age must go through a similar routine, daily events, and so on. Upon parting company, they would not know any more about their respective situations, unless they consciously talked about it. Such a thing is unimaginable between a *galantuomo* and a *cafone* of the South. At first sight, they would recognize each other for what they are and would mutually avoid each other. Foreigners have noted more than once that a cultured Italian feels a greater affinity with someone of the same status who is French, German, or English than an Italian of a lower social status. This is even more true for the South than in any other part of Italy where a caste system is not as rigid and the differences are much more adaptable.

The most noteworthy characteristic of this type of bourgeoisie was its disdain for manual labor and, in general, any form of physical exertion. Using one's arms to earn a living was considered a state of humiliation, a kind of slavery that indelibly branded anyone who had to resort to such work, no matter what the painful circumstances. In a village of the South, there was nothing more pathetic than the sight of a *galantuomo* who has fallen so low that he is forced to live by doing manual labor. Those from his own class avoided the poor man who pushed on dispirited, head down, as others secretly pointed him out to those unfamiliar with the environment. This bourgeoisie had nothing in common with the bourgeoisie of more advanced parts of northern Italy, where work was honored and respected and where, when the occasion arose, the landowners, executives of companies, and the well-off in general did not sneer at bending over. Much like China's upper class Mandarins, the *galantuomo* did not have to do anything with his hands. This attitude worsened the more you continued toward the outer regions extending to Sicily where the disdain for manual labor was so intense that it recalled that of the warrior age of the Arabs from which such a sentiment was derived. Respectable people who fell into conditions of extreme poverty decided to join the *mafia* not out of real criminal instincts but because they considered it the only means that would save them from the abomination of manual labor. The Arab conquest of Sicily and the attitude of *spagnolismo* are the most responsible for the distortions of character and the peculiar psychological tendencies of the southern personality that were the least appealing to foreigners and to Italians from other regions. The aversion to physical exertion, which disrupts the dignity and the pompous seriousness of the person, extended to sports. We believe that in Italy the greatest resistance to the renewal of sports promoted by fascism, a passive and crafty resistance, came especially from southern middle and lower middle classes. It is amusing to peruse, when it appears in front of you, the diatribe of subversive militants—and we are talking about the most intelligent ones and those held in high regard by their followers—against the sports fervor that is seen in all parts of the world.

They are amusing above all because we know them and we recognize them as coming from the southern petit-bourgeoisie. These terrible renovators of society speak like a good country parish priest of fifty years ago. They haven't forgotten their origins, nor has a subsequent subversiveness succeeded in uprooting altogether the dominant ideas in the class from which they come. While this class did nothing but rail against the ignorance of the *cafoni*, it was largely responsible for their state of ignorance. We remember very clearly the tirades of the *galantuomini* in the cafès and in the various social clubs against the schools that disseminated corruption and unbalanced the town's budget. The latter ended up being too drained for the *galantuomo*'s activities. We mentioned schools: they were dark, foul smelling flea traps where the poor little schoolchildren ruined their eyesight, breathed badly, and little more than the alphabet was beaten out of them. Ultimately, the liberalistic middle class did not want to educate the popular classes whom they distrusted and feared and, in doing so, conformed to the original bourgeoisie that emerged from the French revolution and considered "The Fourth Estate" an enemy. The *galantuomini* who complained about the ignorance and the crudeness of the *cafoni*, while doing nothing to reduce it and make it disappear, complained also about the poverty in which those wretches lived. They could not pay for a doctor, nor a pettifogger, nor the local taxes. Lacking any economic sense that was characteristic of a type of medieval caste, they were incapable of seeing that a class of people, who has been milked of every last penny and who has been left with no source of income, was not able to pay for anything. It has no other prospect but to become even poorer, impoverishing in turn the remaining social categories that are closely linked to it.

* * *

In essence, the southern bourgeoisie considered the peasants as basically a conquered race that needed to be squeezed with shrewdness and forced to its last drop of vital energy, leaving them with only a few rags for clothing and a piece of bread to feed themselves. The most generous *galantuomini* made a small charitable contribution to ease their conscience. The *taillable et corvéable a merci* plebes of before the French revolution continued to exist in the South. The *galantuomini* did not have a very clear sense of their feelings nor did they bother to understand them. The most violent and oppressive even denied that the *cafoni* had any feelings or physical sensibilities similar to theirs. Being nearby when misfortunes have befallen both adults and children of the lower classes, the *galantuomini*, without emerging from their customary apathy, just shrug their shoulders and repeat the usual antiphon: after all they are *cafoni*! Tormented and exploited since time immemorial, the *cafoni* expected nothing from their masters; what's more, they did not want anything from them. They distrusted any endeavor, proposal, or initiative that came from the *signori*, even those well-intentioned. When the itinerant teachers of agriculture were established, it was no cakewalk to convince the peasants to attend the lectures. It seemed impossible that the *galantuomini* would invite them to something in which money would not be taken from their pockets or they would not be duped in some way. The popular classes always remained passive, refraining from giving the slightest support to the political and social endeavors of that minority of *galantuomini* who disinterestedly strove for the peasants' welfare and redemption. Because, to be fair, we cannot forget that, out of the haughty and lazy bourgeoisie that we described, there emerged the great figures of the Neapolitan Republic, the Revolution of 1848, and the Italian Risorgimento of 1860. However, the *cafoni* wanted nothing from the *galantuomini*, not even when they were called Mario Pagano,[2] Luigia Sanfelice,[3] Carlo Poerio,[4] Luigi Settembrini,[5] Carlo Pisacane,[6] and Sigismondo Castromediano.[7] The recent history of Italy will never be understood if one does not consider the hatred and distrust that any undertaking attempted by their eternal oppressors instilled in the popular classes. By just keeping in mind the brutality of such feelings, we can appreciate the often-criticized predisposition of our people: the apathy and inertia that were sustained during the half century of attempts to restore the Italian nation. Only then will the ill-fated expedition of Sapri and that of the Bandiera Brothers[8]

---

2   Francesco Mario Pagano (1748-1799) was a jurist, philosopher, and key figure of the Neapolitan Republic of 1799.

3   Maria Luisa Sanfelice (1764-1800), also known as Luigia Sanfelice, was from a Neapolitan aristocratic family, who became a heroine of the Neapolitan Republic of 1799.

4   Carlo Poerio (1803-1867) was poet and activist during the Risorgimento.

5   Luigi Settembrini (1813-1877) was an important literary figure and patriot of the Risorgimento.

6   Carlo Pisacane (1818-1857) was another key figure during the Risorgimento, who was killed leading the ill-fated Sapri expedition against the Kingdom of Naples.

7   Sigismondo Castromediano (1811-1895) was from an aristocratic family near Lecce, who was accused of conspiracy against the Bourbon monarchy. He was elected to the first Italian Parliament.

8   The brothers Attilio (1811-1844) and Emilio Bandiera (1819-1844) were nationalist revolutionaries who were executed during the struggle for Italian

be fully understood. The peasants, who rushed the two insurgent bands savagely massacring them, only saw in such actions a cabala of *galantuomini* that aimed to suppress the King and take over sole control. They considered the King their lone protector. In this, they resembled the Russian *mugik* who looked to *the Little Father* as an infinitely good being who, if he were close by, would have protected them from the harassment and tyranny of the *bojardi*. But he was too far away, they would say sighing, and he could not have known how things were. The camarilla who surrounded him prevented him from doing so. The Bourbon kings and the common people understood one another: they spoke the same language, they had the same tastes, and the same antipathies. Ferdinand II and his plebs joined together in an unforgiving hatred that they harbored against the *pennaruli*, that is the educated bourgeoisie. Ferdinand IV wrote to his wife Maria Carolina: "we can only trust the plebs." All the Bourbon kings based their power on the plebs. And they did well to trust them. It was the peasants who, upon the fall of the Neapolitan Republic, rushed to swell the ranks of Cardinal Ruffo, Gaetano Mammone and Fra Diavolo, winning back a kingdom for the Bourbon dynasty.[9] In Naples, the peasants carried out the *Santa Fede*. In 1848, an indifference and popular hostility isolated the *patriots* who ended up in prison, in exile, on the gallows, or killed on the barricades. The rural element of the provinces, from 1860 to 1865, kept alive the political brigandage of the Borjes, the Donatello Croccos, the Ninco-Nancos, and numerous others who bloodied the southern regions in the mad attempt of Bourbon restoration. This was not an exclusive phenomenon of the South. When Radetzsky returned triumphant to Milan after being expelled during the "Five Days" insurrection, the *barabba* crowded around his horse acclaiming and professing their loyalty to him: "we were not the ones who drove you away, Sir Radetzsky," they said to him in their dialect, "it was the *signori*." And Radetzsky responded paternally: "I know, I know, my

---

independence.

9   Cardinal Fabrizio Ruffo (1744-1827) was a royal vicar of the Neopolitan kingdom and led a royalist-popular counterrevolution against the French under Napoleon. He was joined by the bandits Gaetano Mammone and Michele Pezza, who was known as "Fra Diavolo."

children." Unfortunately, this was true.[10]

The first task of the Liberal governments, as soon as Italy became a nation, was to tackle the discrepancy between the two classes that considered each other enemies. Dissolve misconceptions, alleviate suspicions, have them come closer together, and make them gradually less dissimilar. However, the same components of these governments came from the imperious, bombastic, and quibbling bourgeoisie who, despite tacitly having immortal principles, were convinced that the peasants were irredeemable. The separation remained profound. They were two different races even physically, as demonstrated by anthropological studies of the poor classes. With the continuation of the latifundium, malaria, and agricultural labor, the peasants of the South fell into the condition of the *fellah*. The impoverishment of the rural classes was followed by that of the bourgeoisie who became even more resentful, greedy, and vindictive. It subconsciously blamed its downfall on the *cafoni*, who were the primary cause of all the misfortunes that struck them. Envy and jealousy were targeted against the *cafoni*, especially if their work and activities tended to prosper. They needed to be blocked in every step toward progress and made to look ridiculous in every attempt to refine and educate themselves, or to become civilized.

* * *

And then the exodus toward the New Continent began. The governments of the time should have controlled this massive phenomenon, stem the bursting emigration tide, select its elements and direct them where they would have been able to produce the best outcome for their own welfare and that of the entire nation. Perhaps, once it was decided, emigration was necessary. In Italy, there was the need for the circulation of capital, the movement of money whose shortage was cause for catastrophic sufferings and hardships. However, the lack of understanding of the leaders was simply monumental not to say criminal. They only saw in this phenomenon a good opportunity to

---

10   Joseph Radetzky von Radetz (1766-1858) served as governor of Austria's Kingdom of Lombardy-Venetia from 1850 to 1857.

get rid of the most cumbersome, disturbing, and turbulent element. Worse yet, it appears that it was their intention to dump the national burden on the New Continent. Convicts, "idiots," "cripples," diseased persons, and those intellectually handicapped who are the illiterate: the passage abroad was facilitated for everyone. This freed leaders at the time of a number of responsibilities. In their negligence, they did not realize, or did not care enough about, the discredit that was brought upon our country and of the bad reputation created by sending that element least capable of representing it all over the world. We will address separately the subject of convicts in a subsequent chapter. After all, they were able to manage better than the others and were not the ones to be rejected at the disembarkation in the United States. Instead, paupers, the illiterate, the *feeble minded*, and those suffering from trachoma were immediately rejected. In 1914, the year in which immigration to the United States reached its peak at 1,218,000 with arrivals from all parts of the world, those rejected were approximately 33,000. Keep in mind that the American immigration laws of the time were still very lax. Those barred entry for absolute pauperism or because they were considered capable of being a burden to public charity numbered in all 15,715. Of these, 2,215 were Italians, that is 14 per cent: then there came the Irish, Jews, Russians, etc. Those barred entry for mental deficiency, that is the insane, "idiots," the feeble-minded, "imbeciles," and epileptics amounted to 1,274. Also for these the largest percentage was provided by the Italians, approximately 55 per cent, comprised almost entirely of *feeble minded*. Those rejected for contagious and loathsome diseases totaled in all 3,253: four fifths of these were infected by trachoma. In this category the largest number belonged to Italians as well, with the highest percentage of 18 per cent. They were followed by the Polish, who were a distant 10 percent, and then all the rest.

During the period of our greatest migratory flow, social medicine in Italy was very rudimentary. One bright day there spread the strange, unexpected news—strange for our bourgeoisie and unexpected for our leaders—that America rejected the immigrants affected by trachoma. Trachoma? What was trachoma? Of course, specialists knew what it was. However, in all those years that Italy had been united as a nation (we're not talking about the early Middle Ages) trachoma had been allowed to spread unobstructed into the southern provinces, disseminating boundless misery. In this sense, the lands of the South did not differ greatly from those of the coast of Africa or of Asia Minor. It was common to run into people of all ages—the sight of children made you wince—whose eyelids were reduced to bloody sores. The cases of blindness resulting from the disease were numerous. This horrible fate was accepted without complaint, with a sense of resignation as if it were God's punishment. What perpetuated in the South was the dark age of superstition owing to the criminal indifference of those whose responsibility was to spread the knowledge of how to protect oneself from physical ailments and to make the treatment and results of scientific discoveries available to all. And illiteracy! What strange ideas were those of the Americans to reject anyone who had not attended school! As if the natural condition of man was not to be illiterate. And to think that everyone should be able to read and write! This was the thinking of the *galantuomini* who did nothing about trachoma or illiteracy. As always, they just stood watching, skeptical and chattering, without moving a finger, without pressuring the political leaders and insisting that they modify the intolerable conditions. And the government also did nothing. The few and occasional measures did not change the state of things. The poor *cafone* had to get by as best he could. He took care of his own eyes and learned to read on his own. He longed to emigrate, make money, be productive, raise a family, and get away from the intolerable oppression. Paying out of his own pocket, he hired private tutors who would hammer the alphabet into his head, hardened by time. He sent his children to public school with an urgency never before seen. Even the women learned to read and write. All this in order to emigrate. Worried about the large number of folks who returned to their village after incurring the large costs of the planned emigration because they were rejected by the American doctors at the port of entry, they began to devote as much attention as possible to their eyes. Before moving, they wanted to be sure that they were cured of the disease. They endured long treatments that were necessary for long neglected chronic cases: treatments that often required amounts much too overwhelming for their economic means.

An eye doctor could not always be found in their place of residence: they did not trust the general practitioner. They undertook daily trips of several miles on foot to travel to nearby towns where there was a doctor who *understood*. And the treatment was carried out. The day in which they *passed* the medical exam in the port of embarkation, which for the South was almost exclusively Naples, was a day of celebration and triumph. This is only said here in passing—and it is not very honorable for those who controlled the fate of the town and for the class of *galantuomini* in general—that the most powerful impetus toward health and sanitary improvement as well as the intellectual development of our race was a result of the American immigration laws. It was their dreaded measures that drove both the ruling classes and private individuals interested in expatriation to devote more rigorous attention to the infectious diseases and to put an end to that destruction of the spirit: illiteracy.

IV. THE FAILURE OF THE BOURGEOISIE

The *cafone* emigrated because he was tired of poverty. The conditions of a laborer condemned him to this poverty, making it impossible to obtain a piece of land to work on his own and also to escape from the arrogance and abuse of the *galantuomini*. Initially, these *galantuomini* thought about emigrating as much as taking a trip to the moon. Eminently rooted and traditionalist, they only felt comfortable in the restricted limits of the social class to which they belonged. Not gifted with a spirit of initiative and adventure, they needed to walk familiar roads that gave them a sense of protection and security. Outside of these, there was chaos, the unknown, and the undermining of every value based on birth right. From their brief visits to the city for urgent needs, they returned terrified. No one knew them, no one called them Don Tizio or Don Caio,[11] no one doffed his cap as they passed by. What world is this? Back to the village, back to the village, where everyone knew one another and where everyone enjoyed the respect owed to one's rank! They began to consider emigration with the same fear that one has who is about to jump into an abyss and only when they felt the earth under them swept away. The villages began to empty with the population of some reduced by half. The exodus had acquired an irresistible impetus with its great numbers reminiscent of the ancient transmigrations of peoples. With the blind instinct of a mob, the professional *galantuomini*, merchants, landowners in ruin, clerks and ex-clerks, and that specific category of ne'er-do-wells typical of this class—that is those people who beyond their *galantomismo* owned nothing and did not know how to do anything—followed passively the masses in that ethnic relocation that at times assumed the appearance of an escape.

But they had no intellectual preparation. And yet a solid preparation was indispensable to help understand certain experiences and the strange, unusual, and dreadful aspects of the new environment that they were about to face. Such a preparation would have made the crisis of adjustment less painful and much shorter and would have facilitated, in one word, the process, at times comical, at times tragic,

---

11   Tizio and Caio are common placeholder names.

of transplanting oneself in a new land. The prevailing education in Italy during that time was a classical formation. They continued the medieval humanistic tradition that had been bastardized by German teaching methods. The so-called classical education was reduced to a matter of grammatical constructions. After bidding adieu to middle school, students would still hear ringing in their ears for quite some time the famous professorial question: how do you construct? As for serious studies that would be of service in life, little or nothing. The teaching of modern languages was basic at best. In certain cases, it would have been better had it not existed at all. Having never heard a word uttered from the voice of an Anglo-Saxon, a large majority of English language instructors would teach an imaginary pronunciation based on the idea they had formed studying the so-called theoretical rules.

Anyone who is experienced with English can well imagine what would come out of this. Geography was considered a less important subject and the method by which it was taught generated disgust. Anyone who endured that torture hated geography for the rest of his life. After eight years of accusatives and ablatives, the young students who came out of high school had no precise idea of how those blessed Greeks and Romans ate, dressed, and organized their daily lives. And the student, after several years of torture in geography in which he was inexplicably forced to fill his head with a list of mountain chains inclined in a northeasterly or southwesterly direction and rivers that turned left after turning right, was not sure of the language spoken in Brazil or if the United States and Canada formed one country or two separate countries. With this formidable store of knowledge, for the *galantuomini* it made no difference if they went to New York or to Buenos Aires. Their choice for a new residence was often by pure chance. It depended on whether they had in one city rather than another a *compare*, that is a relative who tentatively encouraged them to immigrate. As far as any knowledge about living conditions in Rio de Janeiro, Tucuman or Philadelphia, it was all the same to them. They were going to America. This was no different from the peasant women who urged a fellow villager leaving for Boston to say this and that to a son, who was specifically in Rosario Santa Fè. Wouldn't they have seen each other in America? The problem was that they didn't know the language. How and why people who studied and possessed degrees would have left for a foreign country in which they planned to reside for many years, ignoring the basics of the language spoken there, remains an almost inexplicable mystery. Moreover, these people did not count on adapting to live anywhere; however, they expected to prosper there, advance, and become rich. To think that someone could realize all this without knowing the language is one of those absurdities that boggles the mind. It's as if a wave of madness had struck that part of the educated bourgeoisie who decided to emigrate in those years. It was a senseless idea that caused an infinite number of tragedies and endless pain. But, notwithstanding its senselessness, a reason can be given for such a way of thinking. The *galantuomini* saw that many *cafoni*, without even knowing how to read and write in their own language, were able to create extraordinary economic positions in the new world. "Imagine what we will be able to accomplish!" they concluded. They paid no attention whatsoever to the language. Language? What does language have to do with anything? Is it necessary to know the language to go to America? However, as we shall later see, the case of the *galantuomini* is very different from that of the *cafoni*.

If they had at least possessed noteworthy skills of adaptability and versatility, an open and tolerant mind, rich in human warmth and capable of accepting without excessive prejudices and antipathy a way of life that was so different, perhaps language would not have been the extraordinary handicap that impeded any progress of the bourgeoisie in the new land. An accommodating disposition and a touch of humor would have contributed immensely in smoothing out the conflict of certain contacts, in resolving painful and ridiculous situations that resulted from getting accustomed to new forms of co-existence, and in accepting different customs and a different way of feeling and thinking in social and family relationships. It was also necessary to have a strong, sturdy and well-trained body that is used to intense activity and hardships. Nevertheless, because of the insulated and restrictive lifestyle of their villages governed by rigid customs full of real moral and social taboos, the *galantuomini* developed a narrow-minded personality that was unreceptive to anything new and was extremely intolerant. Anything that was not *like it was in the village* was a source of disappointment and irritation, and put them in a state of exasperation that bordered, in some cases, on obsession. They began by detesting the form and color of the houses from the moment that they set foot on American soil. They then became disgusted by the appearance and way of dress of the Americans and would explode in rage when contemplating the independence and carefreeness of the girls in the New World. They were prone to a gloomy melancholy and were at the mercy of a chronic irritation that manifested itself by fiery explosions of anger concerning discussions in which their aversions and biases were in some way affected. Not that they were very often wrong with regard to the many things they criticized. What they were lacking was a sense of perspective and historical understanding. In a new country that was still only a few decades removed from its pioneering days, taste, culture, economic, judicial, and civil institutions still found themselves in a formative phase. There was a coarseness, a barbarity, and a lack of *ubi consistam* which bewildered those coming from countries with a centuries-old civilization. But they did not understand the tragic situation in which they ended up. If they wanted security, protection and stability of social order, they should never have left their hometown. It was a contradictory, absurd, and ridiculous situation in which all their invectives against their adopted country returned like boomerangs to those who had hurled them. And why did you come here? And why did you stay here? These were the questions that left them easily deflated and to which they could not respond convincingly. In other words, they should have immigrated to America with a pioneering spirit, without deluding themselves into believing they could find a social system that would protect them, assure them ample earnings, would spare them of any losses, and would accompany them with much ceremony to the ship when they were prepared to return home with their pockets full. But they did not have a pioneering spirit because they also lacked the physique of a pioneer. Their disgust for manual labor and sports had weakened their fiber. They suffered severely the hardships and the lack of comforts they were used to. The process of acclimation, which was difficult for all living things, was especially difficult for them.

They ended up closing themselves in a circle of hostility and hate against a relentless environment that annoyed them on all fronts. The *galantuomini* should have opened those ghettos called *Little Italy* and released their fellow countrymen, urging them with their words and actions to spread into more sanitary and wholesome environments. They were, instead, the most determined to entrench themselves there, rejoicing in finding there the surviving elements of the Italian provinces that, in the home country, were rapidly changing and disappearing. They enjoyed lingering in the local barber shops, in the country-style pharmacy, in a small café where one could find a cup of espresso and Italian pastries, just like in the old country. They would take pleasure in crossing the busiest streets of the neighborhood to meet their friends and chat, wander around the stands in the open market that reminded them of old Naples, participate in the religious processions and colorful parades, and listen to pieces of opera performed by an orchestra stationed in the middle of the street. All this reminded them of the good old days of the festival of the patron saint. Nothing wrong in this if not for the fact that by throwing themselves head over heels onto a nostalgic a way of life so distant from their present reality, they lost sight of the gigantic and teeming world in which they lived and they only looked at the small pockets of foreigners with odd customs as if they were a camp of Indians. However, the enormous world in which one needed to launch oneself with a courageous spirit of pursuit and adventure was of no interest to them. They did not have the weapons needed to take it on. First and foremost, they lacked the language. They put all their stubborn anger in not wanting to know and speak it. They offered the excuse that they had no natural inclination to learn languages. The truth was that they hated the world in which they had come to live. They hated it for a number of reasons, the main one being that it reminded them every second of the position of privilege they had lost. They also hated it because it required emotional and physical efforts that their long stagnant intellects and their bodies, weakened by idleness, could not support. They needed to acquire new ideas, innovate their own culture, and interpenetrate with the spirit and history of a new people. But this required a tremendous effort that they did not feel themselves capable of undertaking. They preferred to utter that they did not want to know anything about America because it was not worth it. After all, what is there in America? Nothing. And for them, there really wasn't anything. As a result, you had professionals who in thirty years of residence in the United States never went to a theatrical performance, as if no American theater existed. There were others whose knowledge of English did not exceed thirty words, and still others who rarely ventured beyond the three or four little streets they would daily roam. It was precisely these people who emphatically continued to repeat: what is there in America? Nothing. The nothing was that they did not see reproduced in the new land those customs that reminded them of the most glorious period of their life: when they were students in Naples with their little seamstress nearby and the hubbub up there in the public gallery of the San Carlo theater.

It was to be expected that those of such a nature would one day or another see their own family members rebel against their tyranny and intolerance. Their children, around whom they had created a vacuum and who continually heard spewing forth insults against the land where they were born, chomped harshly at the bit. And having reached the age of reason, they became aware that those who had put them in the world were foreigners. They did not speak the same language, they did not have the same tastes, above all they did not have roots in the same soil. These children heard their country reviled by these foreigners and, consequently, they discovered in them each day new moral, intellectual, and even physical dissimilarities making them alien to the world that they loved and in which they grew up. Between children and parents there rose a barrier of hostility that slowly transformed into hate. If the children were endowed with a feisty nature, they would explode in open rebellion against the paternal impositions that often resulted in irreparable rifts. While suffering terribly, others with a more submissive nature did not dare challenge the wishes of their parents nor avoid a type of antiquated and absurd education that was inappropriate to the environment in which they had to live. What emerged, especially among the females, were hybrid beings who were pathetic to look at, because they lacked athleticism, educational refinement, gracefulness of manners, all of which were indispensable for them to feel at home and become an integral part of the society in which they were destined to move about and establish themselves. At first contact with an Italian-American family, a quick glance and a little banter among the various characters are enough to understand their situation or give one a glimpse of the hidden drama that unfolds within. In some families, the parents are good-natured, open-minded, and in perfect harmony with their children. These parents rejoice in the progress of their children in various American activities: sports, work, and entertainment. When necessary, they make an effort to speak in an appalling English of which they are the first to laugh good-humoredly together with their children, who love and respect them, notwithstanding their terrible English and their Old World habits. The youngsters see that their parents love them, are interested in them, and do not impede their aspirations. Above all, they do not commit the enormous error of condemning or making a mockery of America and everything American. This was enough to endear them to their children.

But in the families of the category of the *galantuomini* described above, things are quite sad. The father does not let any opportunity go by, whether it be in the living room, dinner table, or car, to curse America or make a wise crack against the customs and institutions of the country to which they have immigrated. And the oldest son, who attends high school, rolls his eyes full of resentment. It is obvious that he is restraining himself from making a scene out of respect for the visitor. There are times when he refutes his father with harsh words, by slamming a book, getting up hastily from the table, and muttering words that are far from respectful. And it is this same father, supported by the mother, who rudely asks his daughter to explain certain actions and how she spends her time, scolding her harshly for having gone to a dance and returning late. They disparage and make insinuations against the company she keeps and the friendships she has made. They make fun of her affections, her passions, and her favorite *hobby*—and all the American girls have a hobby, be it *social work* or the latest theory of psychoanalysis, theosophy or the *rumba*, skating, or the redemption of "negroes," futurist art or motoring. These are ways to give vent to youthful exuberance. They are infatuations that will no longer be around at a mature age. They are diversions whose healthy function will never be fully appreciated: that of distracting the young psyche from concentrating exclusively on sex. However, the parents do not understand. They include in their hate all that is not *like in the village*, all that they have found different in the new land, all that differs from the educational systems in which they were raised during the prolonged Middle Ages when women were prohibited from looking out of the window and marriages were arranged by relatives. They make fun of the girl's passion for tennis, the new diet she has started, and the books she has bought: they make her life unhappy with an unrelenting prod applied to the kidneys, covering her in a cilice full of animosity and incomprehension that shatters her sense of self and is not the last cause for numerous tragedies of youth. Children and parents remain separated by an icy plateau that an entire lifetime would not be enough to overcome. The youngsters do not resent very much the reason behind the reprimands; rather, it is the harsh, overbearing, disrespectful, and offensive tone that is used. Especially the girls resent it, in a country where they are accustomed to expect kindness, respect, thoughtfulness, and civil behavior even by the closest of relatives. One inconsiderate, harsh, and rude word is enough for the young women to lose all respect and devotion to their elders even if, down deep, there remains a little affection. The worse consequence of all this is that the youngsters born and raised in such families develop an instinctive and unyielding hate regarding anything that has to do with Italy. Judging from their parents, they form the idea that it is inhabited by people with primitive habits, limited intelligence, a narrow mindedness, intolerance, dominated by prejudice, shortsightedness, and enduring customs and traditions that the civilized world has long abolished.

Another consequence is a result of the *galantuomini*'s inability to adapt to customs and the new environment and to learn the language. This inability to adapt to ideas and ways of life that were different from those to which they were accustomed was a result of their unwillingness and reluctance to *blend in*, as they say in America, i.e. not feeling comfortable with people with whom one is unfamiliar, act how they act and become, in short, one of them. The Americans judged an entire Italian population by a class that, in its own country of origin, was in a state of distress and represented only the remnant of a Middle Ages that lingered on in the South longer than in any other place. They labeled the Italians as *unassimilable*. It was one of the most serious indictments when the famous law against immigration was debated. The *unassimilability* of the Italians became axiomatic. The Americans asked themselves if these people, who represent the educated portion of the country, exhibit a staunch resistance to integrating into the communities in which they live by restricting themselves to the life of a tribe, what would the others be like? The Americans, as they often did regarding us, reasoned incorrectly. They did not even recognize the warm humanity of our people. As would become evident later, our immigrants, who display a calmness in the midst of adversity, a sense of balance, and an eternal vein of good humor and sympathy toward any aspect of the multi-colored American population with whom they come into contact, have succeeded in making themselves welcome and even cherished by all those who are without racial prejudice and whose spirit has not been embittered and poisoned by a propaganda of defamation and slander.

* * *

It was natural that, considering their mentality and education, the bourgeoisie who immigrated could not take an organizational or leading role in the new land. After an initial moment of disorientation and shock, the newly arrived *galantuomini* to America were suddenly struck by the reality of the situation. In America, they meant nothing. It was the *cafone* who counted. This revelation was like a lightning bolt. All those ideas of self-importance that had endured from the age of reason suddenly collapsed. The *galantuomo* was deeply offended and humiliated. There surfaced in his mind, and it magnified over time, a state of rancor against those who had gotten the better of the undermining of class values and against the land that had caused this phenomenon. However, for the former master there was something worse than counting less than the former peasant: he absolutely needed him. Without the *cafone*, the immigrant *galantuomo* would have found himself in the condition of a new-born child. He could have been in a state of despair due to hunger and cold in the gutter of a street and no one would have noticed. It was the *cafone* who took him by hand at his arrival, guided him, gave him the first instructions, and put in his head the first ideas of how to live and manage in his adopted country, and… fed him. The poor *cafone* did it with respectful and somewhat ironic goodwill as a result of the reversal of roles that had led him, the former employee, to become the protector of his masters. To understand all this, it is necessary to explain further the condition of the immigrant bourgeoisie, both intellectual and non-intellectual, in America. The only degrees that had a certain value, in the sense that they could lend to earning a living in a relatively short time, were those that were health related. Physicians were able to manage sufficiently well. They were followed at some distance by pharmacists and veterinarians, provided they had their papers in order with the law by validating their Italian degree with a state certification exam before an American exam board. The time needed to regulate their position was indefinite: it ranged from a few months to a few years. It depended on a number of circumstances: the age of the person and his mental agility; the knowledge of the language and the amount of time that he could dedicate to the study of English texts; the failure or reluctance to appear at the exams; the greater or lesser ability to assimilate what was new or different in the exposition of scientific theories, methods of technique and professional practice that he observed. The Anglo-Saxon mentality is very different from the Latin one. The rational processes are not identical, and it requires a long, often painful, effort for the intellect of an Italian university student to master completely the methods of scientific instruction that are prevalent in the higher learning institutions of the Anglo-Saxon countries. There is the strange case of Italian specialists, some of whom have received a Ph.D. habilitation in Italy, who have failed the State exams precisely in their declared specialty. They simply did not understand the questions to which they had to respond in writing. It was not that they were ignorant of the literal meaning in the linguistic sense; instead, it was the deep scientific meaning that escaped them. In other words, they were not able to grasp what response was expected of them. During the period in which the health care specialist worked toward obtaining an American degree, there were two options: either he brought over with him a certain amount of money that would allow him to await the results without experiencing serious hardships, or he needed to earn a living the moment he stepped off the ship. In the latter case, the physician was compelled to practice secretly, always at the risk of being caught and brought before a judge and answer to a charge of illegal practice. The pharmacist and the veterinarian, who knew the language well enough to avoid the most embarrassing situations in their practice, adapted by finding employment as assistants for regularly licensed professionals.

Even in these situations the help of the *cafone* was invaluable. He was the physician's first patient upon the latter's arrival from the old county, regardless of whether he had an American degree or not. For the old physician, all that was necessary was the knowledge of his long service in his native village, while for the young green-horn physician it was the fact that he was the son of the local doctor or belonged to a prominent family of *galantuomini*, or simply had an Italian degree, which the *cafone* valued much more than an American one. And the old peasant was equally generous with advice and assistance to the new arrival. He gave him free publicity by singing the praises of his miraculous cures, which was often invented on the spot by a fervid imagination, and he lent him the money to pay the exam fees and set up his office. He also helped the pharmacist, who had not yet earned his American degree, open a pharmacy by becoming its most regular customer and by persuading as many friends as he could to become customers as well. Outside of the medical degrees, all the others were not worth anything. Not even that of an engineer. At first glance, it was almost incredible to imagine that in a country where construction activity was growing at a dizzying pace, an engineering degree was worth nothing. But this can be explained. Construction methods were different and, in all types of large American companies, it was not so much the degree that counted but rather it was rising from the lowest ranks and moving up the various stages of production. If the required abilities were displayed, one could eventually reach executive and managerial positions. In the multiple branches of engineering, it was necessary, as they say colloquially, to pay one's dues by doing a certain amount of manual labor and by being ready to do it each time the occasion presented itself. In some professions in America, the intellectual and manual work are generally not so rigidly separated as in Italy or in Europe. The need for detested manual labor represented, therefore, a relentless nemesis to the bourgeois graduate of our universities.

It is better not to mention the other professions. Why the devil the lawyers came to America and what hopes they had in earning a living and prospering is a question that remains unanswered. The same can be said for the professor of humanities. With the rare exception of someone who found a position in a middle school or high school at a time when in America there was a limited number of those knowledgeable in classical languages and similar fields, for the most part it was a painful *via crucis* of intellectuals who were forced to take on jobs that were below their qualifications.

The same could be said for those with degrees in agricultural sciences, commercial sciences, and social sciences, who did not find a way to apply their knowledge. Then there were the elementary school teachers, as well as the numerous agronomists and surveyors, who arrived in America with the vague hope of finding gainful employment in an eminently technical country and who, instead, found all doors closed due to the differences of methods, the hermetic sealing of technical organizations that were not easy to penetrate and, above all, the language, the language, the language. Moreover, there were the hordes of intellectuals and so-called intellectuals without any clear talent and no specialty in any theoretical or practical field of knowledge: students who had interrupted their secondary and university education due to misfortune, incompetence, or recklessness; ex-officers and non-commissioned officers of the military, *carabinieri*, and finance police who had voluntarily left their careers or had been dismissed; pencil pushers of provincial newspapers; pseudo-scholars and pseudo-artists who descended into America with the fantastic and presumptuous idea to take it by storm (they considered it a country of barbarians) and become suddenly rich and famous. There were also small merchants and small owners of ruined lands, not to mention a number of the above mentioned ne'er-do-wells, and those whose only occupation in the old country was that of *galantuomini*. When the fantasies vanished, the first faint dreams of a career and also—why not?—of splendid marriages in the American world, the immigrant bourgeoisie found themselves face to face with harsh reality. And the reality was this: if they did not want to be blown away like dried leaves, the *galantuomini* had to replicate the way of life of the *cafone* and grab onto their only lifeline: the *cafone*. They had to hold on tight to the *cafone* in a form of symbiosis that for them was a question of life or death. None of the above mentioned professional or intellectual categories, not even the most fortunate, was capable of earning directly from the American economic system. We won't talk about the few exceptions that are too infrequent to invalidate the general truth. The only one who was capable was the *cafone*. All that the bourgeois immigrant earned: money for lodging, food, entertainment; the subsidy for the family left in Italy and the bank savings, all came from the hands of the *cafone* who remained the only intermediary between the American economic system and the rest of the Italians in the home country or abroad. For many *galantuomini*, this, as we said, was an extremely cruel blow and, consciously or subconsciously, they refused to recognize the true essence of the phenomenon. They ranted and raved endlessly against a land where real merit was not recognized, where such outrages were possible, where those with a degree, a diploma etc., etc., had to count on the miserable earnings from an illiterate *cafone* who was raking in the money. In the old country, the *cafone*'s tipping of the hat would not have even deigned a response. The petulant, annoying, unjust, and malicious recriminations escalated like a swollen torrent, were never ending, and continue to this day.

However, the more clever members of the bourgeoisie did not get lost in such grievances. As soon as they realized that *their America* had to be the *cafone* and that the latter represented the plentiful bosom of their prosperity, they immediately got to work. There was the tacit password of *give it to the cafone*. Thus began one of the saddest and shameful periods of our colonial history. It began by the harassment of the *cafone* in every way imaginable. With a boundless inventiveness, traps, snares, and decoys were set with the aim of stealing the *cafone*'s earnings, taking every last cent from him, and leaving him forever penniless, thus forcing him to return to his doomed life. The cynicism of those who consciously devoted themselves to this venture was revolting. Professionals and businessmen confessed the following: "We are unable to gain anything from the Americans. The only one who can do so is the *cafone*. One needs to take all the money that he has. If we don't take it away from him, he'd spend it badly in some other way. The *cafone* does not deserve anything. He's stupid and ignorant. When he gets rich, he becomes impudent. He needs to be kept under wraps." These cynical comments that the old immigrants recognize all too well are nothing other than the revelation of the prevailing feelings of the old southern bourgeoisie regarding the more humble classes. And it was then that the job agency opened by the bourgeois country boor, after having extorted a dollar of *bossatura* from him,[12] found the poor, "unskilled" laborer a bogus job. After a few days, the naïve laborer was fired and, unaware of the criminal organization, returned to the same agency to pay for another dollar of *bossatura* for a similar job. Sometimes he would be sent to break ground or lay railroad tracks in semi-wild places, without shelter and protection, only to be abandoned in the open countryside deprived of any means after the company had cheated him of what he was owed. It was in those years that the *banchista*,[13] also a *paesano*, opened his letters and took possession of the meager dollars that he naively secured there so that they could be sent to his family. These were all small distractions during the process of conceiving the master stroke: a total collapse that would have allowed him to seize at once the savings of the depositors who trusted in his honesty. And it was also during those times that the poor *cafone*, for all the necessities of his life, from marriage to baptism and from illness to death, found around his neck a *galantuomo* who, after having hounded him relentlessly and having meticulously bled him to death with all the pretexts and in all circumstances, both happy and sad, finally offered him a casket.

Instead of finding in his educated fellow *paesano*, advice, sincerity, and good faith, he found deceit, duplicity, and wicked plans aimed to rob him. If he was about to plunge into an abyss, instead of finding a friendly hand being extended to save him, a shove would accelerate the final tumble. So it would be, coldly and with no regrets. Many

---

12   A job fee.

13   The term employed at the time for a private banker.

bragged about the hard blows that they inflicted on a *cafone*. The entire centuries-old hate of an inept class against those who proved to be able to prosper and take advantage of the opportunities that a virgin continent offered came to the surface. The *cafone* was treated like an enemy, a kind of savage against whom it was not worth adopting methods of combat used by civilized people. Any weapon was good. No blow was ruled out. Fraud, deceit, hypocrisy, open violence. All was acceptable to rob, impoverish, ruin financially and physically this new "Red Indian" called *cafone*. Taking advantage of his inexperience, apprehension, and reluctance to enter into negotiations with the Americans who had business methods infinitely more honest than the improvised village businessman, they made him pay a hundred for what was worth two. It was either a luxury cost or a fee for medical services. He was sold things of no value, which he purchased with the utmost good faith, such as crumbling houses and building plots on which a large city would rise. However, the land was still in marshlands. It is incredible how many people the *cafone* made rich, how much money was extorted from him with the most flimsy pretexts, how many streams of cash that flowed from his strong arms were lost in crazy and ridiculous ventures. When the *galantuomini* wanted to launch a campaign from which they would have drawn a major, if not exclusive, advantage, they knew how to handle his soft spot: patriotism. Even though in the fatherland he had known only poverty, suffering, oppression, and disappointments, this admirable product of our race maintained an everlasting and nostalgic love for the home country. And, he gave, and gave, and gave always without hesitation and without scrimping. Shouldn't the money that went to Italy have been used to alleviate the harshness of tremendous catastrophes and improve, through some worthy endeavors, the homeland? And the *cafone* gave: to the Red Cross, to the earthquake victims, to the schools and monuments, to education, to sports, to war, to fund the losses from bad crops, to churches under reconstruction, and to construct new roads, to public works and private charities. For a certain period, he helped reinvigorate the national economy with his support, which amounted to a half a billion a year. He gave continuously with enthusiasm and tireless generosity, without complaining. But he did not always give wisely. Moreover, he made a number of con men rich and filled the pockets of numerous opportunists who knew how to touch a sensitive chord: patriotism. Poor *cafone*! He was not educated enough to distinguish which were truly endeavors of national interest and which were endeavors that benefited some shameless charlatan. And besides those established residents, there descended into America fortune hunters! They descended above all in the post war years when, with greater contacts during the war time, America was *discovered* even by those who first disparaged it as a country where the bums would go. And who didn't get on board in those times! Founders of war orphanages that didn't exist, promoters of monuments that would have never been erected, inventors of marvelous machines, decrepit singers, actors and cabaret performers who had enjoyed a moment of notoriety a half a century earlier, old high school professors who gave lecture tours among their fellow provincial compatriots to sing the praises of their region, builders of imaginary churches and even of universities to be constructed in small towns: all with amazing plans, all invoking patriotism loudly, all with the sole idea of getting as much money as possible from the *cafone*. They had discovered the mother lode! And the *cafone* helped everyone. He gave food to everyone and filled the empty pockets of everyone, whether it was someone deserving of consideration or some greedy con artist. He would enthusiastically accompany them on shipboard on their return home and even invite them to return. Certainly, upon learning of the pitiful end of his money, he felt rather badly. However, with the admirable composure that distinguished him, he immediately got over it and was the first to laugh at it, showing a sound and spontaneous sense of humor in referring to the embarrassment and the ringing words of the character who had pinched him with such ease. "What can you do?" the kind *cafone* concluded philosophically, "he too has to survive."

With the closure of immigration and the *cafone* no longer allowed to enter, who was there to keep things afloat? Businesses of all kinds, be they commercial, industrial, or financial, which seemed to move forward on their own, deflated like an empty bladder. A thriving professional clientele vanished, offices closed. In some a gun shot could be heard. Stores, pharmacies, restaurants that counted on an

Italian clientele are dying. The streets of some Italian neighborhoods have, in large sections, buildings in which not even a soul is left: dirty, collapsing, with broken windows, the ground floor shops look like mortuary enclosures. It seems like the population has been swept away by a plague or a massacre. No one disembarks at the *docks*. No one talks any longer about improving things, risking new ventures, or taking on other careers. The old immigrants, above all the *galantuomini* who in former times were at war with the *cafone*, are crushed, struck by a deathly sadness. They know that America, *their America* has ended and will never return. What's to gain from moving, what's to gain from doing anything? They cast desperate glances at each other and keep quiet. Perhaps in their conscience they feel some remorse. And deep down in their mind they invoke, with a desperate cry, what was once the object of their hate: the *cafone*! The *cafone* who fed them, who allowed them to progress and prosper, the *cafone* who formed the basis for their existence.

In place of the hodgepodge of superfluous and useless monuments to which the *cafone* has contributed with his money, justice would be to build a monument in the Italian neighborhoods of America or in the homeland, a monument more worthy and more noble than any others that would epitomize the struggles, sufferings, evolution, and the emancipation of the real founders of the Italian communities in the New Continent: a monument to the *cafone*!

V. THE *CAFONE* FINDS HIS WAY

The sufferings that our immigrants had to tolerate in the first years after their arrival on American soil were incredible. They had to live in the worst dwellings that had been condemned by the health board: dwellings that had no electricity, no air, no toilets, and often no water. Like infected pigsties, they were exposed to all kinds of diseases caused by the crowding and by a terrible climate in which hot and cold extremes alternate at such a speed that it becomes almost impossible to take the necessary precautions to protect one's health. The humiliations and mistreatment by violent ethnic groups with a crude mentality like the Irish were their daily bread. Moreover, traditions and ideas of the period of slavery persisted in many parts of America and the last arriving foreigners were, in a certain sense, destined to fill the place of the "negroes." In the mining camps of the interior and in the construction and railroad ventures, they worked under a peonage system, watched over and subjected to violence in the event they attempted to abandon the encampment. Gifted with a physical stamina, they were able to compete successfully with the giants of the Nordic race who were much stronger but were affected by organic deficiencies that negated their advantages and made their service unreliable. Our laborers, our peasants, and our artisans ended up being appreciated for their innate qualities of seriousness, for their work ethic, and above all for their temperance. In one word, you could count on them. On the contrary, the northern Europeans' work force fluctuated continually in terms of numbers. Those huge hypoborean beasts simply got drunk: they needed to get drunk, and the next day or so following their drunken stupor no one talked about going to work. It was especially true on Monday to hope that an Irishman, a Swede, a Pole, or a Russian would show up at his everyday job. The Italians were sure to be there. The building contractors began to prefer them to the others. This sparked jealousies. More than once, by taking advantage of regulations in force in some states that required only American citizens to be assigned to work on local and state public works, those who resented the employment of Italian laborers on a large scale were able to have our workers terminated. For the contractors, it always ended in a near disaster. Forced to recruit the Irish and others of northern origin, the jobs proceeded slowly and irregularly, with glitches or they halted altogether. In a state of despair, they had to run to the authorities to have the ordinance withdrawn. It was what it was, the good Northerners worked for two days and were drunk for four. The Italians, citizens or non citizens, had to be called back in a hurry.

Don't think, however, that the battle fought to establish themselves in the American work place did not leave, over its course, an endless trail of dead, injured, disabled, of those impaired in body or mind. Among all the efficient and healthy people that the American Moloch insatiably raked in with its monstrous metallic arms, a large number of them were sent back to Italy weakened by tuberculosis, poisoned by social maladies, paralyzed by rheumatisms, and restricted by heart disease. This made up for the small number of those who were able to go to the New Continent, even though they were not gifted with a perfect body. The Americans exaggerated, as they are known to do, the impact of an inevitable phenomenon during times of turbulent immigration. However, with a typical lack of consideration for everything that concerns foreign matters—one of the more notable aspects of their nature—the Americans have never given much attention to the world and to the multitude of poor devils who left the world of pipe dreams each year after having endured the stranglehold of a brutal and inhuman production system where what counts is the quality and quantity of the item launched on the market and not the feeling and thinking human being who has contributed to its production. Guided by an unfailing evenness and common sense combined with the scent of a bloodhound, the Italian laborers, without anyone showing them the way, realized immediately some of the advantages that the new country offered and how to profit from them. The major problem was to live as cheaply as they could in order to send their families as much money as possible. Many of them decided to live together: they would find empty, shabby residences with very low rent and would then make then as livable as possible by obtaining second hand furniture and by cooking for themselves. They noticed, quite surprisingly, that the Americans (in those times) did not eat the internal organs or the extremities of the butchered animals that were then sold for nothing.

They could, therefore, buy for just a few cents the heads and feet of the calf and pig and any kind of internal organ. They prepared them according to the best recipes of their regions, which ended up being feasts. They were used to vegetables, which were scarce. Consequently, they began to plant them wherever they could find a piece of available land: in the *yard* behind the house, and even in flower pots. It was not difficult for those who lived in the countryside. In the markets of the Italian neighborhoods, one saw for the first time edible products that were unknown to Americans and made their eyes open wide. Old peasant women discovered in near proximity to the city that there was an abundance of chicory: not exactly like ours, but very similar. One could see them bent over in the fields of the suburbs intent on cutting it and filling their sacks. In the evening they returned to the city, leading to delightful scenes with the streetcar operators.

In a foreign and hostile world, they felt the need to protect one another and, therefore, group together. But not having in the forefront leadership groups that would show them the way to form powerful organizations for the good of the majority of the Italians in America, they had to rely on their judgment and experience that, on this subject, were not very extensive. They reproduced on American soil the only form of association that they had known when they were still in their homeland: the confraternities of the various churches in the native villages. There arose, based on these models, the Societies of San Rocco and of the Madonna della Neve, the Cross and the Coronation of the Virgin Mary, and the patron saints of all the villages. Gradually other societies were added that took their name from the actual villages: Roccabella di Sopra and Roccabruna di Sotto, without counting those that were subdivided into two or three for people who were born under the same bell tower of a modest cluster of rustic dwellings. They were inevitably jealous of each other and their local allegiance was so petty and narrow-minded that it prohibited them from seeing anything beyond their own village. In other words, they represented all the defects of a still medieval Italy, an Italy of regions and factions, a still un-unified Italy from which they had departed and of which they could not conceive another ideal and national formation. Many immigrants were veterans of military service. Their patriotic spirit, quite confused and misguided as it was for many at that time, inspired the need to establish an enduring memory to the period spent in the armed forces of which they were proud. They also looked with deep nostalgia at those years that captured the memories of their youth. Consequently, this gave birth to military societies: the bersaglieri and carabinieri, the artillery and cavalryman, the infantry and grenadiers. In many of them, all members held ranks: captain or lieutenant colonels, for example, with the president a colonel or a general. Those military societies! They represented a nightmare for the most educated Italians who were able to judge what a mockery they made of our country in general. One was quick to sneak away when crossing the path of some of them. It was certainly not pleasant to see a little old, bow-legged hunchback drag himself painfully along in the filthy uniform of a bersagliere or cavalryman, with pants slipping off and with a feathered hat or helmet askew on a slumping head. The worst was when they rode an ill-fated nag on which they struggled to remain upright! They had become an amusement for the Americans who roared in laughter as they watched them parade by. But it is also true that the military societies surrounded our communities abroad and our institutions at home in a grotesque atmosphere of a comic opera. It is not that such performances were unknown in America. The impression our immigrants made was nothing new: the Americans had seen something similar in those of other ethnic groups. The Scottish strutted around with their skirts and bagpipes; the Irish in comical half top hats with a green ribbon and riding boots; and the Germans in branch-covered *jager* hats. However, being in the country for a longer period of time, they had greater sense: in the public parades, they chose athletic types who cut a nice figure in their uniforms and they rejected those deficient because of age or because of physical shortcomings. When our by then sizeable number of immigrants began to imitate how the Europeans who had preceded them acted, the military societies were about to end. They remained the only ones to continue a practice that had already faded away, drawing the attention of those who had nothing better to do than make them the object of insults and scorn.

The Societies, no matter what type they were, had very modest goals: provide aid to members who are ill or unable to work and make funeral arrangements in case of death, relieving the surviving family members of costs that were anything but small. Given the scarcity of means, the ignorance, and the narrow-mindedness of those who founded the societies, one could not expect them to be motivated by spiritual and cultural goals and aspirations. They were primitive forms of associations that responded to the instinctive need to meet and gather together in a foreign land. Only in relatively recent times have associations with larger numbers and a stronger financial backing emerged that enjoy more extensive programs with a more dignified tone. At least that was the intention. However, in practice they did not do much more than handle funeral arrangements for its deceased members, which represents their greatest concern and their most notable activity. No comparison is possible with the powerful associations of other immigrant groups that support cultural and educational institutions and construct impressive buildings that become meeting centers for the instruction of social relations, athletic training, and linguistic and literary development. Furthermore, such associations exercise an enormous influence on American politics and make their weight felt in any situation the United States enters in active relations with their country of origin.

* * *

Tossed by a fate much stronger than any of them into an unknown land, the poor *cafoni* initially groped their way in the dark. There was no hope of assistance from anyone. This was especially the case of their homeland government. In the consular offices, the *cafoni* only found arrogance, incomprehension, contempt, aggravation, excessive costs, and criminal irresponsibility. This was true even during the years of war when the consular staff was still permeated with a Masonic-Socialist *virus*, a *virus* however that did not alter the *galantomesca* mentality. The *cafone* was always the pathetic being who was constantly mistreated and kicked around every time he was a nuisance. How it was possible for the pro-socialist bourgeoisie before the advent of fascism, and particularly the southern bourgeoisie, to reconcile the broad humanitarian ideas it championed with a tenacious aversion of the *cafone* that it did not even have the decency to conceal or lessen in some way is one of the mysteries of those times. And it is also one of the contradictions of the fascist era. Because if a number of people belonging to the *galantomesco* type by mentality or by class hastened to increase the ranks of fascism, they did it solely to keep at bay the damned *cafoni* who were raising their heads too much. This occurred in the homeland, but it happened even more in the colonies where the *galantuomini* have even more resentment against the *cafoni*, who, having attained a certain economic independence, no longer have any regard and much less respect for their former oppressors. In their small-minded mentality of incorrigible reactionaries, the *galantuomini* mistook the fascist regime for a type of castigator that would have kept the riff-raff where it belonged. "Now we'll show them these damned *cafoni*!"—they seem to have said in their hearts. They couldn't see, nor were they capable of seeing, the extraordinary social renewal produced by fascism. Nor were they able to comprehend how fascism aimed at the advancement of all the social classes, by striving to eliminate illiteracy, by making poverty disappear, by giving everyone an education and a decent home, by protecting the workers from employer abuse, and by giving Italy a more developed tenor of life in which the largest part of the nation that carries out the most vital work in agriculture and industry is not reduced to the condition of a *pariah*. Now the *cafone* was an annoyance even when he rushed to enroll in the ranks of departing soldiers who were off to defend the homeland during the World War. He was a source of irritation because he dared to arrive at the office after hours. These were the only hours that the poor soul had free after completing a full day's work to support his family. It was unheard of to arrange for a more convenient hour. Abuses, therefore, to this *nuisance*, to this intolerable pest who had the gall to go and get himself killed after hours! He was mistreated, beaten up, and tossed around from one place to another, from one office to another like a bundle of rags. Having learned from their bosses how to be a little tyrant, even the aides soaked up the system: they found pleasure in tormenting, wearing out, humiliating, and treating as a thief this crude peasant who appeared confused and embarrassed, turning his hat in his hands, and who did not ask for anything but to be sent off to the threatened frontline of his homeland.

Nor could our immigrant worker hope for assistance from those of the bourgeoisie who had followed him. He had abandoned his native home to free himself from their domination; instead, he found them again on his back like a swarm of locusts. However, at first, he could not completely get by without them. He could not speak English: he had to tell the history of his illnesses to a doctor and to his fellow country pharmacist. The American professionals did not understand him, had no patience for him, and had no time to waste on him. So it was if he had to buy a home or a piece of land, purchase furniture, open a store, send money home, or have his children and wife come from Italy. He needed an Old World mediator for any activity he had to do. It was a sense of subjection extended to America as a consequence of having been a victim in his homeland. It was only when the *cafone* began to set himself free from the immigrant bourgeoisie that his progress became steady. Time was needed and total freedom was secured through his children. For a family of laborers, having children, even very young ones who were able to express themselves in English, was good fortune. An American who entered into the home of the immigrants for whatever reason—salesmen for commercial businesses, Public Service employee, representative of the Department of Education or Public Health Service—did not even try to speak to the parents. He spoke directly to one of the children on hand: "tell your father this or that" or "explain to your mother that this is the situation." The young boy or girl was proud of being an interpreter. It was both comical and endearing to watch small children attempt to translate into the crude dialect of their parents. The little offspring born and raised in a foreign land served as guides and interpreters for their elders. The shy and backwards women of the southern regions, who were always on guard as if the entire world was plotting against them, began to open up and gain confidence. Consequently, in the company of their children, they ventured into the American stores, those gigantic stores full of large shop windows, escalators, and revolving doors. First they just dared to look at them from the outside with a great sigh of desire and rejection, fleeing hurriedly off for the small purchases to the foul-smelling little shops of a *paesano*, where they would pay two or three times more than in the large stores for the merchandise they needed. They had taken a major step! From then on, these women were able to declare with pride to their friends: "my children take me everywhere. They speak English." And it was from then on that our workers slowly separated themselves from the infected agglomeration of *Little Italies* in order to distance themselves even further, in places that they had never been before and devoting themselves to jobs and challenges completely new to them. Gifted with a greater sense of adaptability than the *galantuomini* and accustomed to physical hardships through which they acquired the strength needed for a life of sacrifices and difficulties, they achieved success in areas so different and distant from their original activity that would make one almost shout "miracle." One could see from their efforts that these workers from the lowest of classes possessed potentially the ingenuity and the versatility that had never before been acknowledged nor not even imagined in their homeland. It is not so much in the cities as much as it is in the small towns and rural regions, or in the remotest of areas, that one finds the greatest surprises. Some examples would be those of a cobbler turned developer of large buildings, an illiterate peasant farmer in a large town not far from New York who lends his name to an entire street made up of all his buildings, an "unskilled" laborer of the rail system who founded the best hotel in one of the most popular beaches in the southern states. One finds everywhere our former *cafoni* and their offspring who, as wide-eyed children, made their first trip in the holds of crowded vessels a quarter of a century earlier. They have the best fruit markets on the Pacific Coast, they own car dealerships throughout the Appalachian mountains, and are owners of restaurants, theaters, and movie houses. In the mining regions, it is common to find former miners who have become mine owners. In some regions, they have total control of the important commerce industries, such as fish and fruit. Some have become kings: we might mention the king of bananas[14] and the king of peanuts.[15] Fishermen from Puglia

---

14   Antonio Cuneo, a native of Piedmont, came to the United States shortly after the Civil War and became to be known the "banana king" after cornering the fruit market in New York, specifically bananas.

15   Amedeo Obici was born in 1876 near Venice and came to America at age

go from Florida to Alaska to fish salmon, and fleets belonging to Sicilian retailers transport fruit from Central America where they have plantations. It is not our task here to treat the activities of the Italians in America. We have made these brief observations to illustrate how the former *cafone*, having severed his ties of diffidence and subjection, is now everywhere. Even in the remotest regions of the United States, one can unexpectedly find Italians popping out of nowhere. They are almost always former *cafoni* who end up there through a series of strange adventures or events that could serve as material for several novels. They welcome you graciously with a simple greeting because the quality that remains intact is their sociability. They tell you about their history, which is usually a history of suffering and often of persecution; sometimes it is a history of fantastic adventures without exaggeration or embellishments, making it more lively with a touch of humor that has never abandoned them, even in those most painful and tragic times. In the end, they emerged from a sea of difficulties and hit the road. A road that they would have never imagined even in their wildest dreams, but on which they proved themselves, oftentimes achieving a success that is the envy of Americans with a long line of descent in this country. They achieved success more easily and more frequently than the *galantuomini* because, contrary to the latter, they have always had a great desire to understand American life and to assimilate into it. They did not shut themselves off like growling mastiffs rejecting all opportunities or turning their backs with contempt to what American life offered them. Instead, they observed it, attentively waiting their turn or finding a breach in the solid wall in order to penetrate through it. And they wanted their children also to penetrate it: at school, in business, in sports. They did not disregard these paths nor did they try to diminish them in the eyes of their kids. On the contrary, they encouraged them to find in these areas a position of the first order. They wanted their children basically to take advantage of every opportunity to get better and move forward. Consequently, legions of young Italo-Americans besieged professional careers, industries, businesses, and

---

11 and settled in Scranton, Pennsylvania. He would then move to Wilkes-Barre, Pennsylvania where he eventually became "The Peanut Specialist" and founded the Planters peanut empire.

sports. In the latter field, they have succeeded in capturing important positions, positions that in the preceding generation seemed to be held exclusively by the Irish. There are many Italians who are champions in a number of major and minor sports in the United States. The sports pages of American newspapers are packed with their names. Twenty years ago, you could not find one name. This is owed to the firm commitment of the *cafone* to see that his children participate as fully as possible in every aspect of American life.

VI. CRIME AND IMMIGRATION

The Europeans who immigrated to America in the years preceding the Great War experienced subsequent mental and spiritual stages of adjustment that left them uncertain in their judgment and confused in their opinions concerning what they saw and observed around them. Even the most intelligent lived in a state of mind of shifting sands, in a perpetual seesaw of sensations and impressions that left them without a firm point of reference to get their bearings. They were unable to formulate definite and lasting ideas of people and things. They went from a fanatic enthusiasm for what they had seen today to an exaggerated and unfair contempt for what they would see tomorrow, always searching for a truth that slipped through their hands leaving them more than ever dissatisfied. After having spent their entire life in America, the majority of old immigrants—be they cultured or ignorant, obtuse or intelligent—were never able to escape the spiritual limbo in whose haze they perpetually felt their way, in the vain hope of finding an answer to their questions. They have reached the sunset of their lives. They now have grown, married children, and the third generation is about to embark onto a world teeming with crazy activities and a frightening unknown. However, these older immigrants are still waiting to satisfy those questions that their agitated and restless mind continually pose. Is America a paradise or a hell? Is America's civilization superior or inferior to that of Europe? Did we do the right thing or was it an unforgiveable mistake for us and for our children to come here? It's not easy to resolve immediately such questions. America offers the new and ignorant observer the appearance of chaos. Next to awe-inspiring institutions that have nothing comparable in other civilized countries, one finds barbaric acts that would embarrass "a Red Indian." A gentility of customs that is more internal than outward, a refinement of manners that has nothing to envy in those of the best European classes, an exquisite respect for the feelings of others and even for those of animals whose care can do nothing but inspire admiration, all go hand-in-hand with a primitive ruggedness, a total lack of respect for the rights of others that recall the psychology and action of the *frontier* and the gold fields during the era of the *gold rush*. Only the few who have tirelessly and thoroughly studied the phenomena of the many-sided and strange life of a diverse and immense continent have, in some way, been able to make sense of the chaos and find guiding principles that help them understand contradictory and seemingly incomprehensible circumstances that they run across each day during their life in exile.

One must look for the principle cause of this problem in certain, specific attitudes of the Anglo-Saxon spirit that observers of other races often compile under the generic label of *hypocrisy*. Whether it concerns hypocrisy or a type of innate reserve, the truth is that the Anglo-Saxon does not willingly make public his own shortcomings and anything else that may throw a negative light on his race. While he is always ready to judge harshly other foreign people and customs and to highlight the superiority of institutions and manners of behavior of a people who have emerged from their Albion ancestry, he willingly lays a thick shroud over the historical crimes of which the Anglo-Saxons have been guilty in the past and over the disgrace and degeneration that tarnish life in present times. The foreigner who comes to America finds himself before a closed book. In the early days of his residence, he experiences the illusion that everything is quite the opposite. No newspapers in the world are more extensively informed on every aspect of public life than those in America. In no other country do crimes and private scandals receive so much attention by the press and are reported to the public in all their stages with such an astonishing delight in detail. In fact, one finds that such an abundance of details is useless, excessive, and inappropriate. Only after years of persistent research—and only if the foreign observer has the time and the disposition—does he realize that this abundance of extras serves only in masking the real truth. And the public will never know the truth. In every American occurrence, whether it be political, financial, or administrative in nature, in every case of ordinary news, from the most sensational to the least observed, in every public scandal, in every private tragedy that splashes blood on certain circles of American high society, there is always some intrigue that the greater public will never know. After stuffing columns and columns with any event that has shaken public opinion, the reader of American newspapers is convinced to know enough about the matter.

Instead, he knows only as much as the publishers of newspapers want him know. And that much is very often a small part of what has actually occurred in the secrecy of some secluded alcove, in the living rooms of luxury apartments, behind the closed chambers and offices that, due to the responsibilities and power invested in them, they control the life of the country. There is a type of freemasonry among the American ruling classes. They belong to the political and financial worlds, or simply to blood and money aristocracy. It is a freemasonry that comes to a decision in the tacit understanding that certain truths should never leak out of a tight circle of inducted. If things were known as they truly are, the people would lose all respect of the said classes and the remaining trust in the institutions. Adhering inevitably to such a freemasonry are the judiciary and police in whose chambers acquittals, sentences, and non-suits in a kind of *do ut des* that would outrage the strict European jurists are rigged, decided, reduced, and mitigated.

It was not easy for our immigrants to find their way. Early on, they had to overcome their first impressions, which were anything but positive. Upon their arrival when they had to pass through the ugliest sections of the *docks*, they ended up settling in the poorest and dirtiest neighborhoods of the city. However, they could not help from noticing the beauties and opulence that their adopted land offered. The initial disgust was followed by enthusiasm which, in turn, was followed by an intimate revolt against the atrocious injustice and barbaric acts that the new arrivals had to witness or of which they had been direct victims. And so it remained for their entire stay in the foreign land. In so much moral chaos and uncertainty of judgments, it was easy for the Americans to administer their propaganda of assimilation of this new population and shape it according to their own ideas and their own views. The recipe was simple: all that was good and beautiful in America was the product of the superior Anglo-Saxon race and their Northern kin. All that was terrible, disgusting, and horrible was brought here by the inferior Mediterranean and Eastern races. Among the abominable practices introduced by the newcomers was crime. As one knows, the Northerners, who are of high and noble intellect, abhor such things by instinct and by habit as a result of their bloodline. Those from the Mediterranean and Eastern worlds, who are excitable, vindictive, and prone to crime, have no respect for human life and are ready to destroy it for nothing. The only salvation for someone born in the cursed lands of southern Europe was to absorb the customs and ideals of the superior race. But what it kept carefully hidden was its being one of the most destructive races that has ever appeared on the face of the earth, a race that had wiped off the earth entire native populations and caused the extinction of a number of species of still living animals, many of which existed until relatively recent times. As for the blemish of crime of which they believed themselves to be exempt, we shall soon see the standing of the superior Anglo-Saxons in relation to this phenomenon.

Such propaganda conducted relentlessly in the schools for children and even in those for adults and disseminated among all the social classes through newspapers, magazines, and books ended up having an impact on our immigrants who considered themselves the scum of the earth. And this is what was wanted; to produce in them a type of *inferiority complex* so that they would remain in perpetual adoration and subjection before their Anglo-Saxon superiors and masters and would not dare allow themselves the slightest act of independence. The menace was the Italian: America had to defend itself in every way against forms of new and unknown crimes. The press publicized endlessly the *mafia* and the *camorra* with all the exaggeration, superficiality, and lack of knowledge of the subject, and the deliberate lies that are typical of the American press. The trial for a famous crime that took place in the Neapolitan criminal world was transformed by the newspapers into an event of international importance. If they were to do as much for all the trials of their *underworld*, there would not be enough newspapers to cover them. But what was the situation of domestic crime compared with that imported in the decades in which there flowed into America the masses of our immigrants? Is there any truth to the thesis that violent crime and other criminal acts were unknown to the colonizers of the Anglo-Saxon race and constitute a mental deficiency introduced by the despised Mediterraneans? American society originated from chaos, from peril, and from violence. From its earliest days, the new land became a shelter for adventurers, criminals, religious fanatics, pirates, slave drivers, and derelicts of the worst kind waiting for a stroke of fortune, real and genuine lunatics in the grip of madness. The first Anglo-Saxon colonizers were not the holy men that they would want us to believe but rather people without scruples who were possessed by a thirst for wealth in whatever way it could be obtained. The famous cause of religious and political freedom is a fantasy. The first Puritan colonies that settled in America set out on the great journey drawn by the hope of material gain. The farthest thing from their intentions was the establishment of a society founded on the principle of political and religious freedom. What they wanted was their own religious and political freedom. The various Protestant sects fought each other to death. Not to speak of the non Protestants. A Catholic, whether Spanish or French, who ended up in their midst at the pinnacle of the fanatic period, would have come to a bad end. The great prophet of Puritan intolerance of Massachusetts, Cotton Mather, laid in wait for William Penn and his Quakers as they headed toward the American coast in order to capture them, try them as heretics, and sell them as slaves on the Barbados Islands. The treatment of Indians casts an indelible stain on the entire white race. Without the help of the Indians, the early colonizers of New England would have never overcome the first terrible winters in that region. It was the poor natives who provided them with corn and other food supplies, who lent themselves to the essential jobs of constructing the first wooden villages, and who advised them of the unfamiliar conditions that arose as they settled in an unknown land. In return, they were stripped of their lands, sent back into the virgin forest, and massacred without mercy. The New England sea captains who read the Bible each day with great contrition became rich through the transfer of slaves who were taken on board along the African coast after frightening raids and unloaded in the cotton plantations of the southern states. Piracy was not considered a dishonorable practice but rather a form of legitimate trade. The most respectable people of the Anglo-Saxon colonies were devoted to this trade. Even senior officials armed pirate flotillas at their own expense and entrusted them to the most famous seafarers of those times. Sometimes they did not reject the opportunity to participate personally in one of these adventures and lead it. They would return loaded with spoils plundered in the unprotected coastal cities of the

Spanish Main on which they hurled themselves like a mob of demons massacring and torturing indiscriminately women and children. It was not just the Spanish cities of Latin America that were victims of the pirate attacks. Often the band of pirates attacked Anglo-Saxon *settlements* located outside of the well-trodden trade route. When the leaders of such horrible adventures returned to communities where they were held in esteem, they were congratulated for the successful operation and they acquired greater influence and prestige as a result of their accumulated wealth. At the wedding of one of the most dreadful and disgusting pirates, the famous Blackbeard, the governor of one of the southern states was present.

The abduction and kidnapping of people was one of the most widespread practices in England and from there it proceeded to America. *Shanghaing*, as it was and is still called for similar practices, had various purposes: free oneself of annoying creditors, assure oneself of riches by having an inconvenient legitimate heir disappear, supply a crew for ships with a bad reputation, and find laborers and settlers so that they would plough the unrewarding and insalubrious lands that the British Crown assigned to its aristocrats. In each of these cases, the strategy was the same: using a pretext to lure the victims near the shore where there was an awaiting vessel dedicated to such actions, they would gag them, tie them up, and drag them on board. If the poor devils were destined to be written off, they would be left to die of hunger or of other needs on a deserted beach or they were dispatched without much fanfare to the bottom of the sea. The others, who were to serve some purpose, stayed on as sailors or were sent off to be field slaves, closely guarded and under the threat of being done away with at the slightest suspicious motion. Thousands of people were *shanghaied* on American soil and ended up as *indentured servants* on the large landed estates of their masters. They were a type of serf who was obligated to remain tied to the landowner until he had paid off the burden of a debt for the forced transfer and sustenance. A debt that they were never able to pay. The practice of *shanghaing* has always existed in America and continues in a more subtle way even today. In the fierce struggles for work that exist in the United States, one often hears of organizers who disappeared because they represented a threat to an owner's interests. They are found after several days when the most sensitive phase of the conflict has passed. In some cases, the victim of the *shanghaiing* has been transferred to the deserted beaches of South America. However, other types of abductions were very common in the United States: to extort money, to remove political rivals in the most crucial moments of a struggle, to assure an inheritance or other financial advantages. Sometimes representatives of the various legislatures have been abducted so that they would not be able to vote on issues that are fiercely contested where their vote would have been able to tip the scales. In the more tragic cases, heirs to large fortunes have disappeared without leaving a trace.

When the vast lands and the boundless, free resources of the Western *frontier* were opened to all, as they were during the period of the *gold rush* when flocks of gold-seekers descended from the four corners of the earth first toward the golden fields of California and later toward Alaska, violence became in America a normal way of life and the principal form of government. The competition became ruthless and ferocious. Everyone for himself and God for us all. Woe betide anyone who remained behind, woe betide anyone who did not exercise an ongoing and threatening surveillance of his conquests and treasures. Woe betide anyone who allowed himself to be taken unawares or in a moment of inattention and neglect. In a few maneuvers, he was left stripped of everything and had to count his blessings if he was able to save his life. The *frontier* infused the psychology of the American people with an unbridled individualism, egotism, and violence up to the present day. There followed the hoarding of natural resources by the most powerful and the most cunning who succeed in ensuring through intimidation and corruption the consent, the protection, and the complicity of the political authorities for the creation of their gigantic monopolies. The history of great American wealth is the history of fraud, violence, and crimes. To do away with troublesome rivals, no means were considered illegal. Some of the great captains of American wealth, philanthropists and benefactors of libraries and museums had the labors of their rival companies blown up. During strikes, these leaders and their large companies commonly resorted to the practice of hiring *gangsters* to break strikes with attacks, abductions, and widespread shedding of blood. When this was discovered, no one was surprised. The potentates of money continue to be deemed the pillars of society and the bastion of religion. In the boundless territories of the primitive world of the West and South, there always existed, under various forms, banditry. In the more civilized states of the East, especially in the urban areas, *gangs* have always existed. Ever since the Dutch sat under their *stoeps* in the New Amsterdam that emerged on the lower point of Manhattan, there began to form *gangs* that had a booming life up to the present day. It was stupid, therefore, to talk about the *mafia* and *camorra* as unknown forms of crime on American soil. The United States has always had its banditry, its *mafias* and its *camorras* in the upper as well as the lower social strata. And all the *moroni* of the rascist propaganda should not have made, whether it be through ignorance or bad faith, all Italians look like the demolishers of an admirably ordered society. We said ignorance. Alas, many of the Americans who are the most involved in social and ethnic issues are those who are the least familiar with their country. It is a *cant* that has remained since the primary schools. And that *omertà*! *Omertà*: it is something unheard of! There were people who pretended to keep hidden their own shenanigans and not reveal them to the authorities. Has anything like this ever before been seen? But this was pure and simple anarchy and they, those Americans who were so pure and sincere, did not want to take into their home people whose minds were corrupted by such a destructive moral depravity. Ah, those Italians! When a crime was committed, it was never possible to extract one word out of their mouth! A hundred of them participated in an incident; however, once interrogated, no one saw anything, no one knew anything. Terrible, isn't it? Right. These disgraceful *dagos* acted exactly like the guests of one of the many *parties* of high society or, let's say, of the Hollywood *demi-monde*, where often a death occurs. Go find out from those people how things really unfolded! A revolver didn't discharge on its own, indeed really on its own, striking poor Jim or Joe or Jack directly in the temple? A knife blade didn't plunge accidentally between the ribs of Bob or Dick while he leaned over the table? No one could explain how it happened. What a coincidence! Didn't Gwendolyn immerse herself in a bath dying there of a heart attack? And the strange case of Clarence who, after one drink too many, leaning too far back in his chair ended up hitting his head on the floor fracturing the base of his skull. All one can do is bow politely and apologize to the investigating authorities for the trouble. All unfortunate accidents! Now if this isn't *omertà* we do not know what other meaning the word may have. And why place such a serious charge on a poor, ignorant Sicilian who tries, albeit on the basis of essentially antisocial considerations, to spare a friend any trouble, while wrapping in a courtly aureole the behavior of the guests at the previously praised *parties*? And the actions that link politicians, police, judges and *gangsters*? These are certainly not the despicable organizations that went under the name of *mafia* and *camorra* which, after all, never migrated to America. Their representation was made up of small disconnected groups that acted independently one from the other. Nor were their activities of great importance. Quite something else were the American criminal organizations that circulate around tremendous interests in which the deluge of millions is dizzying.

The truth is that in America not much importance is attached to human life. This can be seen in the ease with which one takes risks. They are often done to show off one's bravura, at times for a bet, through carelessness or excess. Americans are tainted by neuroses transmitted by criminals, by religious fanatics, by hot heads, by hysterics, and by lunatics who populated originally the first colonies and who were bolstered by the numerous half-wits included in the subsequent migratory waves. In a country where each year 13,000 people are murdered, 20,000 commit suicide, and 34,000 are killed by automobiles, one cannot say that it respects very much human life. This is without counting the many who are massacred in the industrial plants, and these are the saddest cases because perhaps two thirds of those accidents could have been avoided had the necessary precautions been put in place to safeguard the life of the workers. Nor does a violent crime make much of an impression in America, in contrast to what the propagandists of racist supremacy want you to understand. And the fact that no one is excessively moved by the atrocious crimes is highlighted by the scandalous acquittals that jump at you each day in the press coverage. American justice, be it that of the judiciary system or that of the court of public opinion, can be compared to the justice which, according to the theory of a famous criminologist, would be women's justice: at first, all the criminals who end up in their hands run the risk of being ripped to shreds, subsequently they are all acquitted. When criminal attorneys who know their craft defend crimes that have aroused public indignation, they have no other concern at the onset of the legal battle but to let the public outcry *cool off*, as they say in jargon, which in itself constitutes an important ploy. After a few months, no one will remember the matter and it will not be difficult to snatch a verdict from the jurors. Violence pervades American life: violence at the bottom and violence at the top. The misdeeds of the criminals find their response in the atrocities of the police. With its *third degrees*, its tortures, and its beatings, the tactics of the American police do not differ much from those of the *gangsters*. And the mentality is the same. The crimes of the Americans of the Nordic race are strange and incomprehensible. They are degenerative type crimes. They are characterized by the absence of a rational motive. Contrary to those committed by Mediterraneans, these crimes lack a *cui prodest*. One kills for the *thrill*, which is to say a new emotion, because some mysterious voices have ordered him, to satisfy strange impulses, to absolve a religious mission, or simply for sadistic purposes. It is always that strand of deep neurosis passed down intact to the new generations by the bloodthirsty and violent forefathers who were possessed by religious frenzy and had fallen prey to *wanderlust*. They were deviants, bigots, and rebels who were eternally urged by the demon of the unknown and adventure.

* * *

This brief overview of one of the most painful sides of American life aims to give due proportion to the crime of immigrant Italians and sets it in the environment where it practiced its activities—an environment that was far from paradise. It also explains how the Americans were not really the most qualified to cast disrepute on all our people, as was done at the peak of immigration, labeling us as half wild and afflicted by uncontrollable, bloodthirsty tendencies. This, however, should not blind us to what are the real problems of our immigration and the stains that obscured abroad the good name of Italy. Italian criminals came to America. And they were many. Unfortunately, they arrived— as we have observed in preceding chapters treating our immigration in general—in the eastern regions that had only recently achieved a state of refinement of customs and material well-being. It was not an idyllic society by any means; however, crime had diminished its malign activities in less ferocious and brutal forms. The inhabitants of the East did not pay attention to what took place in the South and West where crime reigned in barbaric measures. News of atrocious facts were few and rare and those who lived in the more fortunate sections could delude themselves into believing that the rest of the United States was like them. Consequently, the American communities where groups of Italian immigrants settled were frightened by the crimes that occurred around them. In southern Italy, the tradition of brigandage was still alive, as were the structures with which it operated. Therefore, the crime that the criminals from southern Italy transported to America was typically brigandish in nature: a threatening letter asking for sums of cash; abductions, especially of children (this upset American consciousness more than any other thing); the elimination of their prisoners when there is an inflexible non-compliance to communication; the implacable vendetta as the fate that struck those who had betrayed the secrets of the *gang*.

Our southern regions had unfortunately known all these things up to a few decades ago. There still moved about our villages people with their ears cut off, a reminder of their encounter with the brigands. These were the methods that were used by the bandits who roamed about the Silla, in the forests of Monticchio, and in the Vallo di Bovino. When the liberal governments of the thirty year period that followed the unification of Italy boasted of having extinguished the brigands, they committed a small error of assessment: brigandage had not been extinguished, it had emigrated. The killing of women, who were victims of senseless excesses of jealousy in a country where crimes of passion began to be lost among the distant memories of a barbaric past, aroused to the fullest extent possible the disdain of the Americans. There were numerous Italians who, unfortunately, were involved in the white slave trade. It is a credit to the Nordic people that this ignoble kind of crime is almost unknown among them. The Irish criminal, as crazy and corrupt as he may be, would unlikely muddy himself in such baseness. Even the lowest forms of humanity have a chivalrous respect for women and have been educated to refer to her with a sense of almost mystic adoration that they would consider themselves inferior to a worm if they were to drive her to shame and to live off her. They prefer to brandish a rifle and attack a train. There was a time in the years preceding the European war when Italian neighborhoods were shaken by bombings. There wasn't a day that the newspapers did not report the news of houses and stores blown up as revenge, threatening letters sent to the wealthiest and most prominent people of the communities, children kidnapped, and people who disappeared mysteriously. Then there were horrifying cases of people cut to pieces whose grim remains were found in trash containers, children murdered because their parents were unable to pay a ransom, and families destroyed because of the war between criminal *gangs*. One of these incidents was enough to cast such a bad light on our immigration, which was already held in low esteem for many other reasons. It had such a dreadful and terrifying reputation that after many years it is still unable to rehabilitate its image. The small bands of criminals (since it was really only small groups) were encouraged to act by the inaction of the police, who cared very little if the Italians killed each other, by the cowardliness of the targeted victims, and by the American judicial system. They took to signing the threatening letters with the signature *Black Hand*. Thus was formed, and little by little expanded, the legend of an extremely powerful Italian criminal association that covered an immense network of organizations committed to corrupt the entire United States and Canada. The Italian became synonymous with a robber and a *black hander*. Among the American upper classes, there spread a terror of the Italian who took on at times almost comical characteristics. When introduced to important people to whom your not very bandit-like appearance did not raise any suspicion, they would leap backwards hearing that you were Italian. The more ingenuous would let slip out: *But, you look like a gentleman!*

Italian and gentlemen were titles that one would not conceive of being coupled together. There were those who had an interest in adding fuel to the flames and did not let any occasion pass to do so. In the cases of sensational crimes, the press never failed with its glaring headlines to point out even to the casual observers that the author of the crime was an Italian. If the individuals were of other races or

Americans, the news would be handled with a few lines in small print. The statistics were inflated and, in every case, they were not impartial and objective. In the case of the social phenomenon we are dealing with and in order for the statistics to have any value, they must consider the ethnic composition of the human group under observation. American criminologists and sociologists compared the percentage of crimes committed in the American communities with those that took place in the Italian communities in order to conclude that the criminality of our immigrants was much higher than that of the natives. But they did not consider (was it forgetfulness, ignorance, or bad faith?) that in the American communities there existed the normal proportion of women and children whose contribution to crime is almost nothing. Instead, in the Italian communities the proportion of men from 20 to 45 years of age, in the full flush of virility, accounted for, in relation to women and children, as much as 80 or 90 percent. Naturally, that elevated the rate of crime.

All this does not diminish in any way the enormous responsibility of the old liberal governments that got rid of the dangerous and unruly elements by facilitating their crossing to America. All it took was a member of parliament to ask for a passport for a suspicious character, who represented a danger and a threat in his constituency, and a prefect and chief of police would do all they could to oblige him. Tremendously irresponsible, our old leaders bartered the honor and dignity of Italy in the world and the good name of its people for a temporary quiet life. The laziness, indifference, and moral cowardice kept them from taking the necessary measures to immobilize definitively the criminals; instead, they preferred, as the quickest and easiest way, to dump them into the Italian communities. The Americans know these things and they have not hesitated to berate us for this on every occasion. The bad individuals who, with the complicity of officials, escaped from the homeland's prisons found across the Ocean their ideal moral climate. Unleashed among our poor workers who were unable to benefit from any protection nor did they possess any genuine means of defense, they became rampant plunderers of the Italian communities. It was not worth rebelling, complaining, or turning to the law. One could only bow one's head and submit to the most outrageous demands. Otherwise, woe betide: not only was his safety at stake but also that of his entire family. Upon his arrival, the criminal was welcomed by those of his own ilk. While the poor intellectual, who was often without friends and relatives, had to face the tough road all alone, wandering around in the dark, making mistakes, faltering, often falling into an abyss of neglect and poverty from which he was unable to recover, those who belonged to the crime world found in the foreign land an organization. No matter how rudimentary the group, the *gang* or a vaster affiliation, it was always an organization. Unfortunately, it was the only efficient form of association that existed in those times in our communities. The *gang* utilized the special abilities of the criminal who immediately felt strongly protected. He acquired a brass, an audacity, and a boldness that come with impunity. Due to countless invisible strings, the *gang* to which he belonged was connected to an American racket that depended, in turn, on well-placed political figures. The latter used these criminals to promote the vast network of their own financial and political interests and, in return, they thwarted the raids that the justice department occasionally attempted to organize.

Many years ago the murder in a Sicilian city of a *detective* of Italian origin, Lieutenant Giuseppe "Joe" Petrosino, aroused great public interest.[16] Even then there was an outcry against Italian crime. However, when investigators searched the *records* of the criminals that Petrosino and others were able to obtain in Italy through hard work, they had disappeared from the archives. This could not have happened without the powerful interference of American political figures who remained safely behind the scenes. They promote a number of enterprises: they make use of the Italian criminals as physical enforcers. These powerbrokers were the authors, organizers, and financiers. In recent memory, as it was for *bootlegging* so it was for the various types of contraband, as well as for the sensational cases of the counterfeiting of money, there often appeared Italian names. How intimately grateful they must be to the much reviled *omertà* of our immigrants that provides them with the ultimate security! The American judicial system appears to be designed specifically to protect the criminals. There are

16 Lieutenant Joseph Petrosino (1860-1909) was a legendary New York City police officer whose Italian Squad was established to address the Black Hand menace that preyed on Italian immigrants in New York. He was assassinated by the Italian mafia in Sicily, while conducting an investigation.

many legal loopholes, the process is so long and complicated, and the safeguards that surround the accused are so numerous that the lawyers specializing in these issues easily win the contest. They know how to take advantage skillfully of the opportunities presented by the laws so that the criminals entrusted to them do nothing but enter and exit the halls of justice. It would happen that after a roundup of rogues carried out in the Italian communities following some crime or a series of spectacular crimes, our peaceful immigrants expected things to be calm for a while. Instead, what is and what isn't, after a few days the most dangerous of the shady characters, who were believed to be safe behind the bars of a prison, reappeared triumphant and intimidating and acting defiantly along the streets of the neighborhood. Distrust and demoralization followed. It seemed that only a career of crime would lead to success on American soil. It was the criminals who flaunted expensive jewelry and luxury automobiles. They crushed the humble worker with their ridicule and their contempt. And this had a deleterious influence on the youth. As soon as they reached the age of reason, the youngsters could not help but compare the life of their fathers, who were forced to spend hours and hours digging, digging, digging, transporting blocks of stone, and laying down tracks for a few dollars a day. On the other hand, the youngsters who never did anything went around well dressed and dazzled those damned to hard labor with their cavorting, lavish, and joyful existence. And lessons were soon learned. American life is terribly demoralizing for the poor and for the children of the poor. The atmosphere of materialism that permeates it easily leads to crime. Honesty, perseverance, and a commitment to one's job apparently do not pay. The best results are gained from gaming and from an illicit lifestyle.

The United States of America is the only civilized country in the world where the activity of its citizens is divided into *legitimate* and *illegitimate*. From the public's point of view, there is no difference between the two. One could devote himself to an *illegitimate* activity and not lose the respect of those who know him. All depends on what he can gain financially from it. There are many types of *illegitimate* activities that are considerably more profitable than what can be earned from a job with the same weekly pay. Naturally, there are always risks in gambling: *illegitimate* activities can lead you to wealth, but they can also send you rock bottom to jail or drive you to the *death chamber*, where the electric chair awaits you. Both for the natives as well as for the immigrants the temptation is great. There is no other country like America in which the line between honesty and crime is so thin. Many crossed it without knowing it and without thinking about it, moving insensibly on the side of the enemies of social order. It is one of the reasons why some Scandinavian countries do not accept criminals deported from the United States ten years after they have left their native country. They are no longer children of the original environment but rather of the environment that has shaped them in more recent years. But ten years are still too many. Five years of American life in the *slums* of the poor neighborhoods are enough to transform a laborer, who left his country of origin with a clean criminal record, into a person who is no longer very sure of what is right and what is wrong. And it is even worse for the children who are raised in those cauldrons of corruption. They flee from those squalid and dark shacks in order to escape the laments, the misery, and the lack of air and space. They descend into the street where they find other companions of the same ill fortune. They begin to hang around the corners, bother the pedestrians, and pilfer the street carts. It is the initial formation of the *gang*. The *gang* becomes more numerous and more powerful as the boys grow. It merges with other *gangs* and becomes a criminal organization of the first order. Out of it will emerge future *gangsters*, future thieves, and future candidates of the electric chair. This is an outline of Italian crime in America to whose initial development we Italians have contributed with our original transgressions. And it would be unjust and unfair to deny. But it would be equally unjust and dubious not to give due consideration to the preponderant share that American customs, environment, and institutions had in its expansion and consolidation. So that it is understood in its exact contours, it is necessary to consider all the exaggerations and misrepresentations that were the product of bad faith and overt antipathy to our race, to our civilization, and to our history.

VII. THE SECOND GENERATION

The second generation has always been one of the most serious problems for America. No matter from what race or people the children of immigrants come from, the development of their intellectual, moral, and physical nature has been profoundly affected by the uprooting from the original stock, by the displacement to a new land and the resultant crisis, and by the necessity to adapt to a new environment. In the society in which they now belong by a matter of fate, there was no legacy of moral, family, and religious traditions to abide by in cases of doubts and difficulties, and no rules of conduct or ideals of co-existence to guide them. The second generation has always produced the worst criminals, the most dangerous and amoral beings, without feelings, without manners, and without laws; *halfwits* and deviants who have many points of contact with the savage. Even the best give the impression that they are incomplete beings. They may have succeeded in obtaining excellent positions in their chosen careers, and they may have distinguished themselves in their fields of specialization; however, after being around them a while, you sense that they are lacking something. It is an instinctual feeling of which you would be hard pressed to find a concrete example. They are without a component that we would call *humanizing*. It's as if a link of the chain that joined them to their humanity and to their civilization had been broken without them being able to secure themselves again to a new humanity and a new civilization. If the problem was already troubling for the children of northern European immigrants for a number of reasons—first and foremost the disparity between the civilization to which they belong and the one that dominates in the country of adoption—it was aggravated by the arrival of immigration waves of southern and eastern Europe. The Italians were no exception to this sad rule. Having had to overcome much greater difficulties and obstacles than others as a result of their extreme poverty and the lack of organization in assistance and guidance during the early years in America, the consequences of a very sad period fell on their children whose physical and moral personality was embedded with signs of indelible deficiencies. At first contact with the Italo-Americans and their condition, there arises a very strong aversion in the mind of someone who has recently arrived from Italy. An aversion that oftentimes results in disgust and repulsion. Let us quickly add that these feelings are heartily reciprocated. Among themselves, the young Italo-Americans make use of slang to define the various types of Italians with whom they come into contact. The descriptions or nicknames are anything but complimentary: generally they are ridiculous and disgusting. Italians find the descendants of their fellow countrymen to be crude, ill-mannered, ignorant, and intolerable. They lack any sense of refinement, they do not know how to hold a conversation, they do not respect their elders, and they have no other interests besides baseball and cars. The Italo-Americans consider the new arrivals as ridiculous and excessive in their display of courtesy, authoritarian, pedantic, overbearing, and antiquated in their manners and ideas. These Italo-Americans don't give a fig about their culture in the same way that these new arrivals ignore or do not value the greater experience of daily life that undoubtedly the former possess. Such impressions can be minimized through mutual interaction but will not completely disappear. They will always look at each other with suspicion, ready to discredit aspects of the other's character that they dislike most. So begins the tragedy of the Italo-American who, as in the ancient fable, is neither fish nor fowl: he is not loved by those of his race and he is given little consideration by the society of which he has become a part. Proof of this can be found in the fact that an Italian who is educated and acquires his culture in his home country feels more comfortable with a learned American who has had an old world Anglo-Northern background than with a representative of his own race born and raised in America, even if the latter has gained considerable success in finance, politics, or culture. In turn, some Americans prefer to have social and intellectual contact with Italians from Italy than with their newly arrived compatriots. The fact is that Italians and Americans feel part of two great civilizations. Though unlike and often divergent, these civilizations have solid foundations and both have deep roots in a distant past. The Italo-American does not belong to either one. He is a hybrid, a grafting that often succeeds but many times fails badly. What he has learned is limited, pieced together, and half-baked. One can see that it is not an integral part of his personality. It is a cultural and ethical heritage of which he does not feel strongly a part and that he is ready to barter for any substantial profit presented to him. Besides, the Americans know that the Italian from Italy, no matter how poor, has received a family and social upbringing whose strength of principles represents a type of higher education. The large majority of the Italo-Americans come from a *slum*. And traces of the *slum* can never be removed by any level of higher education, degree, or professional success. The *slum* is exposed in the way the politician, university professor, renowned physician, and celebrated attorney express themselves. It reveals itself in the way one dresses, walks, behaves in the ordinary circumstances of life, and by the tastes and tendencies of those who have spent the critical years of the development of their personality there. No sooner do they step out of the area in which they have established themselves, they display a vulgarity, crassness, ignorance, vacuity, and a lack of judgment that tell you how their early levels of education have been formed among the groups of young thugs on the corners of the city streets. There are certain gestures, certain inflections, certain mental attitudes and ways of looking at things that they never lose. For anyone who is familiar with American things, there is no way that one can be mistaken.

Even with social conditions being equal, the difference between those who belong to families in which there remain traditions of sophistication and culture and those who took their first steps among the smelly and garbage-laden narrow streets of the working class neighborhoods is astounding. Such statements are not intended to scorn or discredit unjustifiably the descendants of our ancestors who grow up on American soil. Many of them bring honor to the land of their fathers and the number continues to grow of those who penetrate every branch of American activity and achieve, through their talent and hard work, positions of the first order. The unfortunate situations mentioned above are the inevitable results of adjustment to a very different environment from the one in which their parents were raised. Furthermore, the new American civilization will emerge from the children of this most recent immigration. Not retaining anything of the Old World, these children who, once they have broken ties that keep them only slightly connected to what has remained of the endangered Anglo-Saxon civilization, will give America an original make-up that will not trace its historical, cultural, political, and legal roots to one race. However, it is important to make clear, without any merciful façade and ambiguous affirmations, what is the cause of the tragedy of the Italo-Americans at this time. Because, as we will soon see, it is a tragedy.

Regarding their physical characteristics, the children of Italians born in America can be summed up in two large categories: those who have been raised by their families according to methods in use among the well-to-do American classes and those who have grown up in the poor neighborhoods, in cramped and crowded homes, with an insufficient, inappropriate, and mediocre diet. Until some twenty years ago, Americans had a very bad diet. They ate primarily meat whose consumption has been incredible. They consumed meat up to three times a day with little or nothing else. Legumes and vegetables were almost unknown; in any case, they didn't like them and no one asked for them. Their cuisine was crude, primitive, and lacking in taste and flavor: a pioneer cuisine. One can imagine the effects of such a one-dimensional and little varied diet. The Americans suffered from dyspepsia, constipation, kidney and heart problems, and high blood pressure. One of the most glaring effects of such an unwise diet was their very bad teeth. The children's teeth were really disgusting. It was often the case that youngsters of both sexes around twenty-years of age, who were well developed and attractive, had lost their teeth and wore dentures. The Americans had the worst teeth in the world. However, in the last twenty years, they have made enormous progress. The promotion of a more balanced type of diet has been intense and persistent. This has been done through popular magazines, radio, conferences, and confidential advice of health professionals. There has been an insistence on the reduction of the consumption of meat and sweets, the latter being an area where there has been an enormous abuse. Given the low cost of sweets, American girls did nothing else but chew *candies* all day, losing their appetite and ruining their stomachs. They were advised to make plentiful use of vegetables, fruit, legumes, each of which was highlighted for its special qualities and its positive effects on the organism. Even here the Italians taught them something. The Americans began to study our dietary habits: they praised our cuisine, our crusty bread that is not the mush used in America for bread, olive oil, and the great variety of fruits and vegetables consumed by Italians. Fortunately, around that time, our immigrants began to plant an astounding abundance of these products and the food stands of the neighborhoods in which they lived seemed packed with unknown varieties that left the Americans speechless and curious. During the World War, the draft boards never failed to notice that the Italians who came up for examination had teeth that were much better than those of the Americans and certain other physical qualities of organic resistance that placed them in the front line as human specimens. Studies were done on their way of life and, above all, on their dietary habits. The results were that they used very little sugar and sweets and they consumed, instead, a great deal of fruits and vegetables. Conclusions were drawn from the gathered facts and were circulated for the benefit of all.

Then came the vitamins. In America, knowledge of any kind is never limited to a restricted group of specialists; instead, it is circulated through the most widely varying means among all the social classes, especially if it is information that concerns hygiene and public health. This is a generally accepted claim of the United States that elevates it above countries where scientific discoveries remain permanently sequestered in the hands of bigwigs who guard them jealously like mystical secrets that laymen must not approach. Furthermore, education is widespread, since primary school is mandatory until the age of fourteen. Every mother of a family can be updated on the latest health and dietary regulations that must be followed in the raising of children. Books and special magazines on the subject, all popular in nature, are numerous and widely circulated. The women of the middle class know precisely how many milligrams of various vitamins are needed for a child during the different stages of development. They discuss this at length when they meet, citing the authors from whom they obtained this knowledge and comparing results and their personal experiences. Even the mothers of the poor classes learned, at a basic level, how to manage in the raising of a child, which are the beneficial things and which are things to avoid. This in itself represents enormous progress from the blind ignorance and brutal prejudices of the past millennia. Each mother in America, even of the most modest social classes, now knows that, along with either breast or artificial milk and cod liver oil, the child must have a glass of orange juice every day to avoid rickets and other problems caused by a vitamin deficiency. The results of the adoption of a more rational nutritional regime have been impressive. American youth display a much more healthy appearance than that of twenty years ago and they can now flash magnificent teeth. Moreover, one sees around fewer corpselike figures, fewer hunched shoulders and sunken chests. Our immigrants and their children, especially those hailing from the southern regions, had suffered and were suffering from different organic deficiencies than those that afflicted Americans. There were basically two opposite extremes. While the Americans abused an animal protein-rich diet and made very little use of vegetables, fruit, and legumes, our people did the complete opposite. They consumed abundant portions of these foods but were not in the habit of eating, except for rare occasions, meat, milk, and butter. Even here, the lack of necessary vitamins in development often caused rickets. In terms of a propensity for rickets, there was the humiliation in seeing in American scientific texts Italians classified alongside "negroes." In their original localities, this centuries-old nutritional deficiency, coupled with malaria, had profoundly affected their skeletal development causing the small stature of those populations. It was that small stature and the pitiful appearance that so negatively impressed the Americans who ended up considering us a degenerate race, corrupted by organic defects that would have never allowed it to develop an advanced civilization.

However, it has been splendidly demonstrated in America that this deficiency of stature is not a fixed characteristic of the race. Certain things seem almost miraculous among those immigrants who, thanks to their more fortunate economic conditions and sharper intelligence, have been able to raise children in homes full of space, light, and air, in clean and sanitary neighborhoods, by feeding them rationally during their developmental years and, following the example of the Americans, by using plenty of milk and butter, while not forgetting classic Italian foods, and by having them take advantage of sports.

Giants have emerged from shrunken, almost dwarf-like parents. When you enter certain homes of Italians and the parents introduce their children, you are almost tempted to ask just to be sure: but are they really your children? You're afraid that you may have misunderstood and that they are the youngsters of the neighborhood who happen to be there by chance. Formidable girls with perfect features appear at the door and strong, athletic boys, who are returning all energized from a game of *football* or *baseball*, enter like a whirlwind. And you cannot help but wonder that if they had stayed in their ancient regions they would have had the stature and features of their fathers. This phenomenon we are discussing can be found especially among groups of immigrants who come from an ancestry long renowned for its attractiveness and the aesthetic perfection of the Mediterranean. There are certain young children of the Calabrians, for example, who, when they are tall in stature and fair skinned, cannot be distinguished from the descendants of the Anglo-Saxons because of the dolichocephaly that they have in common. Another trait that in America tends to disappear is the dark color of the Southerner. As a result, not even this is a fixed and distinctive characteristic of the race; instead, it is due only to climactic reasons. Their children, who are born in America, have much fairer skin than their ancestors.

For the descendants of the immigrants who have not been able to benefit from the American standard of living, their history is much more painful. Born and raised in poor neighborhoods, they have grown up as God has willed it. Their father and mother, who had to go to work in the morning, were unable to take care of them. Parents and children are strangers to each other, and often hostile. They do not even have a common language. The youngsters did not even learn the few indispensable words of the dialect to be able to understand each other. They grew up on the streets in the middle of the *gangs*, which we discussed in our chapter on crime. They hate everything that is Italian or smells Italian. For them Italy represents the poverty and the coarseness of their parents, which is reflected in their current state. The physical appearance of this category of Italo-Americans leaves you breathless. Little, deformed, and with putrid teeth, they wear on their face the imprint of brutality and degeneration. The girls as much as the boys. They congregate on corners and their shouts and husky voices make you shudder. They remind you of hardened escaped prisoners. They speak a kind of *babu english*, as they say in India about the English spoken by Indians, and their vocabulary does not exceed two hundred words. They look stupid and are prone to insults and threats. Their intelligence has remained atrophied, as have their feelings. They have no affection for anyone, they feel no sense of obligation toward anyone, and they do not respect or obey anyone. They fear only the laws of the *gang*: it is their book of law. If their parents had remained in Italy, they would have become honest peasants and expert artisans. Here they will become criminals, *gangsters*, and subject to hanging. At the most, they will remain dead weight without ambition, without will, without faith, and without ideals. In thousands they wander around the working class neighborhoods. When they are seen intent on doing nothing but planning some malicious act, you can't help but reflect upon the criminal negligence of those whose business it was to create organizations dedicated especially to remove these children of our race from the streets and direct them to healthy environments. For example, they could have been sent to the rural areas, where they would have become useful to themselves and would have garnered the respect of the American communities and honored the land of their fathers.

* * *

The condition of the Italo-Americans is tragic. A large majority of them are unaware of this. They sense a moral discomfort but are unable to explain it or they attribute it to other causes. However, a minority, gifted with a more lively intelligence and a keener sensibility, is able to determine perfectly the reasons. We are speaking above all about the Italo-Americans of the middle classes or those who, despite not originally belonging to the middle classes, became part of them by virtue of a professional degree or hard earned positions in other fields. They were told in school that America was the land of opportunity and equality. There was no difference of race or creed. Anyone who had the necessary qualities would be able to move forward and recognition would not have to wait. And they believed it. At that age, you believe everything and are trusting and enthusiastic about the land where you were born. Was it not the greatest country in the world, the richest and the most free? Was it not a land without prejudice and without the separation of classes where, no matter what your origins, you were appreciated for what you were worth and what you could accomplish. And as long as the young Italo-American remained in high school, college, and, eventually, a University, things went well. He would attend the classes of American professors, have schoolmates of ancient American stock in which each treated one another on equal footing, and participate in American team sports. Ultimately, he ended up believing himself to be one hundred per cent American. In certain moments, he was even able to dream of having come to America with the *Mayflower*. There was, it's true, the matter of his name which was a little annoying. An Italian name, in some cases five or six syllables, a name that his teachers and his schoolmates did not know how to pronounce. The former tried diligently and painfully to come up with it in order not to offend the sensitivity of the student, but the latter shortened it into one or two syllables. The worst was when the name had a ridiculous or obscene sound or meaning in English. In that case he had to calmly and courteously put up with the rather nasty jokes of the other students and not show his outrage. Otherwise, there was trouble. It was hard not to hold a grudge against his parents who had come to America with such a different name or who could have at least changed it in good time. Besides the inconvenience of the last name, everything else went very well. Then came the years of graduation and of the ceremonial awarding of the degree. It is a moving celebration attended by the families, and the students say good-bye to each other with big promises of seeing one another again. And the new professional had entered into real life. Naturally, his most intense and determined aspiration was to burst triumphantly onto the American scene and make a name for himself. Was he not an American, far away from the Italian environment that disgusted him and that he never wanted to see again? However, much to his surprise, he begins to realize that all his attempts to put his plan into action invariably fail. He gets back to work every time with much good will, always blaming himself for the failure and attempting to correct the so-called mistakes he had possibly made. No, he just could not make a name for himself in the American world. He felt an invisible wall rising up around him that isolated him, rejected him, and sent him back to square one. All of a sudden, he began to suspect that the discrimination, whose existence had always been denied in school, likely existed in practice, if not in theory. He began to reflect that even if he felt perfectly American, the Americans of ancient stock could possibly not consider as such one whose strange surname attested to the recent foreign origin. The attempts were no longer renewed: he needed to live. He needed to return to the place where he had left with so many hopes and so many illusions: to the Italian community that in memory of his father and mother would have given him some bread. With the exception of a few individual variations, this has been until now the typical tragedy of the Italo-American. Numerous and brilliant exceptions do exist, but they are not enough to change a situation that only time will remedy.

If only a small number of children of immigrants are slowly, and with great difficulty, able to penetrate the American economic world, having remained until now on its margins, it is even worse in the social world. One cannot, in all conscience, speak of a deliberate ostracism on the part of the old guard Americans; however, through their actions, it is as if an ostracism exists. Perhaps it is the fault of no one: the assimilation of different races takes place only after a slow and painful process and moral suffering is inevitable for those caught in the period of transition. In general, Americans do not love foreigners and they are neither fond of nor interested in foreign things. Nor do they understand them. This is a very strong trait of *insularity* that they inherited from the English, reinforced by all the years in which they remained closed in their continent. They gave no thought to what was happening abroad and their ideas about the world were vague and obscure at best. Only the World War forced them to leave their provincial shell, where they had hermetically enclosed themselves, and get an idea of other peoples, other nations, of their language and their customs. They accept reluctantly foreigners in their close circles or they accept them on one condition: that their guests behave like them, think like them, speak like them, and act like them. In other words, that they eliminate any trace of exoticism even in their personal appearance and that they forget as quickly as possible that they are foreigners. In this case, we are talking about daily practice, not contacts that occur over an extended period of time on special occasions. In this latter case, exoticism may even be pleasing and the foreigner is exhibited like a rare and strange animal with very amusing habits. For the immigrant whose personality was formed in the country of origin, a complete transformation is impossible. There are too many differences of thought, habits, tastes, and tendencies. When Americans and Italians residing in America come together at exceptional celebrations—festivals, banquets, weddings, and festivities of all kinds, they exchange formalities and courtesies that such circumstances require; however, they will end up separating spontaneously like oil and water. At first, it would appear that with Italo-Americans things would be different. They are born in the same land, they speak the same language, and they have had a similar education. However, if you do not stop at first impressions and observe attentively what happens in American society, you will end up finding Italians on one side, Americans on the other, and Italo-Americans in the middle, separated as if in their own compartments. Of course the categories are not rigid and the nuances are limitless. Some Italo-Americans will prefer to connect more with the Italians than with their compatriots, others feel more drawn to spend time with Americans, acting indifferent and scornful toward those who came from the country of their parents. But, as a whole, the division remains what we have described.

There is a reason why such groupings form and it carries much weight. The social life of the Americans is intense, much more intense than in some European countries in which the contacts are limited to those of the family unit where each one barricades itself as in a fortress. Each refuses to become familiar with outsiders except for business reasons. The middle class, and above all the lower middle class, does not give much attention to building a wide network of social relations because they do not know what to do with them and feel that they are only an annoyance and an expense. In America, instead, there is no social class, from millionaires to laborers, that does not have its *clubs*, its leagues, its *meetings*, with all the entertainment, dances, receptions, and other gatherings. The American society is not a society of castes. It differs from English society, full of innumerable and subtle distinctions between *higher low middle classes* or *lower high middle classes*, which are guided by a precise and scrupulous ritual that does not allow for much movement and interference between one and the other. With the exception of the highest aristocracy of money that revolves around a couple of hundred names and tries to forget its modest and even abject origins by surrounding itself with a solid core of ridiculous and *pitiful snobbery* imported from an *ancient regime* Europe, castes do not exist in America. In certain parts like New England, there was until a short time ago a *brahmin* caste, that is eminent families who for several centuries represented the social *élite*, which was handed down from generation to generation. It was more one of wealth, culture, and high offices and positions to which the maintenance of social order was entrusted. There was another one in the South, the traditional *southern gentlemen*, who represented a feudal and land-owning aristocracy. But if there still exists such castes, they are becoming more and more lost in the memories of the past.

In a certain sense, classes do not even exist, namely those fixed classes common in Europe in which, unless some extraordinary event occurs, the son of a peasant will continue to be a peasant like his father. In America, classes are extremely mobile; a laborer today could become an industrialist tomorrow and, vice versa, the industrialist could descend to the ranks of laborer. Although no fixed classes exist, classes, nevertheless, exist, perhaps as temporary groups that form and dissolve continuously; however, for the period that they last, they have their rules, their etiquette, their social code, their preferences and their antipathies. They surround themselves in an exclusive circle, rigorously establish what can or cannot be done, and are engaged in ostracism. Even in these very mobile classes, intruders were not well regarded. As we have noted, many Italo-Americans come from *slums* and this makes them immediately undesirable. Even in the lower middle classes, there are certain traditions of the old Anglo-Saxon education, traditions of *gentility*, to use an English word, certain nuances in behavior, in the way of expressing oneself and in dealing with others, and respect for celebrations and customs that arrived several centuries ago from old

Albion that cannot be taken lightly. It is enough for an Italo-American to break one of these rules of *savoir vivre* to make him understand that he *does not belong*. But even if there has not been any infraction of etiquette, some human types, just like heterogeneous chemical substances, cannot mix. If on the outside he is American, he has remained more or less Italian in his fundamental feelings. So it is with his temperament, at times hot-headed, so it is with his judgment of human actions, so it is with his opinion of feminine qualities, so it is in love, in jealousy, and even gastronomic tastes. Oh, the Italo-American will be invited to dine with American families, participate in occasional receptions, see every once in a while old classmates from college or university to revisit the good old times of their youth, take part in *parties* and sporting events, but that's it. He will never become one of them, he will not have daily personal interactions with them, and he will not become an integral part of an American social category. He will always remain an outsider with whom one maintains courteous relations of acquaintance. The coldly isolated Italo-American falls back among his fellow Italo-Americans who, alone, can understand what crosses his mind. It is with them that he can express his true feelings with the assurance of being understood even with a simple gesture, not with Americans to whom he is ashamed to expose his tragedy, not with Italians who would be insulted by his failures. And it is from the years at school that his tragedy begins. How many schoolmates are there with whom he has ties of affection and friendship? He hears that the others frequently host *parties* at their homes: he has even been invited a number of times. But he cannot return the favor as much as he would like. He is reluctant and ashamed to bring his fellow schoolmates to a shabby and bare home located in a sleazy neighborhood where his mother, poor woman, does not speak any language, does not know how to host the American way, does not know how to prepare a tea or a luncheon, and just to say the most common things she yells at the top of her voice as if a terrible drama is unfolding or if danger is threatening her guests.

In essence, the Italo-American is a *déclassé*. Even when an academic title or financial position gives him the ideal right to penetrate the American middle classes, he is unable to do so. One cannot be surprised by how even the Italo-Americans who have obtained prominent positions in politics and in their professions remain outside the American social world and how restricted is their circle of friends, which is limited to people of their ethnic group. We are speaking of true friendships, of close friendships and not those that are made for reasons of business or workplace. Evidence of what we are saying can be found in marriages. A young Italo-American generally marries an Italo-American girl. When he marries an American, she is generally from a class inferior to that he wishes to aspire. A physician, for example, will not marry a young girl who belongs to the fine middle classes, but a *nurse*. With this, it is not our intention to cast any shadow on one of the most admirable categories of working women. Perhaps it is the most sensible marriage that, in America, a physician could have. Nevertheless, it is to illustrate how the process of *déclassement* that we spoke about above works. And so it goes for other categories of professionals and businessmen. Nor could it be otherwise. The same difficulties that one finds in the student *parties* mentioned earlier occur in marriages. There is the enormous obstacle of introducing very boorish parents to families of rather high social conditions and a fine upbringing. Even if the girl has modern and open-minded views and is willing to disregard such things, her family would not consent. They would create such difficulties that only a young women determined to face being banned from her society and the danger of being stripped of all her inheritance could overcome. In the more modest working classes, different ethnic groups generally mix more easily. Less smoke, less pretention, less affectation, and no rigor of etiquette. Mutual respect, rough simplicity and naturalness in human relationships. It is precisely from said classes that the fusion of that Babel of races that is America has its origins. The products of such unions who, due to the phenomenon of social capillarity, will rise to the upper strata and will create a neutral ground in which the ethnic groups that have remained intact will dissolve to form the future American people.

Many children of immigrants, however, do not even attempt to attack the American fortress. It seems as if the enormous efforts of their fathers to break away from their country of origin, the painful struggles and the hard labor endured to establish themselves in the new land have imprinted indelible signs that manifest themselves as a type of exhaustion, a lack of energy and initiative that impresses you. They are decidedly inferior to their parents whom they, infatuated by their American birth, in their hearts pity if not scorn. However, they have remained attached to the little shop that the old immigrant set up thirty years earlier, but without being capable of improving it or expanding it. They remained attached to their father's *business* from which they derived the only means of support without providing any personal contribution if not confusion, incompetence, and waste. Others live off the labor of their elderly mother and sisters, roaming from a *bar* to a *pool room*, from a shop to a pharmacy, blurting out nonsense, always full of fantastic ideas, always on the verge of realizing great things that never happen. If they are professionals, no sooner do they receive their degree they take on the grueling task of displaying a sign with their name on the same small window in the same little house of the same neighborhood where they first saw light and where thirty years earlier their "unskilled" laborer, fishmonger, green grocer father stopped. By exploiting the modest family friendships, they find their first clients among those of the same village or region of their parents. There is a sentimentality in simple folks that causes them to support the son of a fellow villager with a certain pride: he is always the son of our buddy Tom or our buddy Dick who has taken a profession in America and does honor to his village of origin. However, for such types of Italo-Americans, there is no West, there is no adventure, there is no risk, there is no unknown. With a fluency of language, it should be easy for them to go out, push themselves toward distant places, and find roads that are untrodden. They remain, instead, doing a miserable and degrading service in their poor native neighborhood from which they will never leave and where they will never make any progress. No real personality of undisputed superiority has yet to emerge from the ranks of the Italo-Americans: financial geniuses, captains of industry, creators of huge productive organizations, inventors of machinery that lead to a revolution in industrial processes, scientists who have linked their names to revitalizing discoveries or applied the most advanced approaches to the scientific fields, artists of genius, prominent writers, intellectuals, philosophers, and critics of wide acclaim. Nor have there been specialists with original ideas in various fields of pure and applied knowledge. Up to now, they have given their best as intelligent collaborators, modest contributors to one or other of the huge industrial-scientific organizations of the country, professionals of above average ability, persons who have made some headway in politics, especially in local politics, and men who have achieved high ranks in the judicial area. There is not much else. The tragedy of the Italo-Americans is that of all *déracinés*, of all those who have been torn from their original stock and transplanted in a new land, in a new environment among new human groups. Many are disheartened and become lost, others, perhaps the majority, settle in with difficulty and lead a miserable and painful life. Only those few gifted at birth with admirable and vital energies and spiritual and physical qualities that put them in a position to adapt, without great effort or serious handicaps, to the necessities of an existence quite different from those of their ancestors will plant powerful roots in the soil. These will give life to the majestic trunk that will remain as testimony to the strength of a race.

VIII. THE CLOSING OF IMMIGRATION

Some decades after the wave of immigration from southern and southeastern Europe had begun to spill onto the shores of the United States, the Americans of Anglo-Saxon heritage, who tightly held the reigns of the country, began to worry seriously about it. The strange hordes that poured into a land that they considered reserved to Protestant Northerners of the English tongue affected them like a barbaric invasion. Their appearance was not very reassuring. They spoke strange and dreadful languages that sounded like *gibbering*, and they had unusual and often dreadful customs. What would have emerged from such humanity when mixed with the original American population? Moreover, the new arrivals were not Protestants. The religion to which a majority of them belonged recalled struggles that still inflamed their blood, episodes always kept alive in the memory of an implacable fanaticism. They inherited from their ancestors the spiritual scars that distorted the mind, and in their ears they still could hear resound the cry of *no popery* of the religious wars. Did they have to bring into their own home the hated *papism*? Did they still have to witness the exhibitions of the *scarlet woman*? And then there were the Jews who rushed onto American soil like clouds of flies. And there also appeared the orthodox Slavs, with their Greek crosses and Byzantine rituals, the vanguard of a mysterious and unfathomable world that was straddled between Europe and Asia, a world of still amorphous swelling masses whom they only awaited to burst the banks. Was the beautiful unity of an Anglo-Nordic population, tall in stature, blond haired, blue-eyed, English speaking, and Protestant, destined to be broken? America's greatness was the work of the Anglo-Saxons. Did they have to give up the control of their land to unknown people who arrived from across the ocean, never participated in the constitution of the nation, did not understand its ideals, and was entirely foreign to the original population in mentality and customs? The Anglo-Saxons saw slipping away from them the position of privilege that they had been guaranteed, the monopoly of power and wealth that they had until then exercised unchallenged and without fear of competition. And when the Anglo-Saxon believes his wallet is threatened or wants to achieve political ends of any kind, he sets forth his ideals. The last arrivals were not capable of understanding American ideals. It would be difficult to say what precisely these ideals consist of. And if one were to ask more precise definitions to those who put them forward, they remain very embarrassed in defining them. The famous ideals materialize into a history of rapacity and plundering that have few equals in the world.

So it is. Having set out to war against the despised immigration, it was necessary to wave the big banner of ideals. As occurs in all campaigns of national importance, the watchword was launched by Washington. In the newspapers, magazines, and books, which were increasing like unhealthy flourishing of poisonous vegetation, there were persistent, relentless attacks, especially waves of assaults against immigration in the last decades. They would not allow for the subject to die down and disappear. Improvised anthropologists and ethnologists set out to explain that all was based on the grounds of race. Never has there been a demonstration of so much carelessness, so much irresponsibility, and so much ignorance on a given subject that because of its seriousness should have been treated with much greater weight than how it was handled by the so-called scholars of history and sociology. These people have cobbled together a competency based on old discredited theories extracted from oblivion, which have been polished and restored for the occasion. The Americans do not have their own culture: they borrow from here and there, as best suits them. Before the war, the German cultural heritage was held in the highest regard, also because there were a great many German professors in the universities. In the onslaught against immigration, there was an attempt to instill a semblance of life in old, moth-eaten mannequins, those mannequins that the Germans periodically pull out of storage closets, as occurred even recently, to impress the naïve and use it as a weapon when they seek to make a name for themselves politically or culturally. The mammoth mishmash of odd doctrines is essentially well-known to all: the Nordic Aryan race, dolichocephalic, blond and blue-eyed moved in a certain period from its original locations to develop great civilizations in the different countries where they settled. Thanks to them, we have the Greek and Roman civilization, the Indian civilization of the Vedas, the Persian civilization of the Avesta, and the marvelous blossoming of the Italian Renaissance. The Nordics are *globe-encirclers*, those who have in their scope the entire globe. The other races belong to the so-called *nativi*, those who do not move from their locations and from whom there is no spark of civilization. To produce something, they need the fertile crossbreeding with the noble race. In any case, one can only expect from the latter lower quality labor of application and reproduction: creation, leadership, and guidance is up to the superior race. Every time that the *nativi* have mixed with the Nordics, their moral and intellectual level has been elevated. However, for the latter it has been a different story: they have been corrupted, have lost their high ideals, and have been weakened to the point of degeneration. In some cases, they have completely disappeared to the point of totally blending in with the indigenous races. It became, therefore, a vital matter for the Nordics to maintain their purity and not crossbreed with inferior peoples if they did not want to face deterioration and death. The countries in which the Nordics dominated were guilty of senseless and destructive politics admitting within their boundaries countless hordes of foreigners who belonged to an inferior *stock* that damaged their intellectual, ethical, and biological essence, causing chaos.

Through age-old experience, one recognizes that it is perfectly useless to demonstrate, both in countries where they originated as well as in those that accepted them, the inconsistency of these doctrines. Serious scholars, not affected by racial prejudice, have gathered in vain proof upon proof to conclude that an Aryan race does not exist, that the Germanic nation, the alleged original location from which the chosen legions set out to conquer the world, is inhabited almost completely by brachycephalic people who came from Asia. And lastly, the so-called Nordics, who populate the Scandinavian peninsulas and the British Isles, instead of being an indigenous race, were a branch of the Hamitic race from which they separated at the beginning of the Neolithic period. This branch distinguished and defined itself during the long centuries in which it remained in the Nordic countries segregated from contact with other peoples by an ice barrier, a remnant of the last great ice age. The insistence on erroneous theories can only be explained by having them be of use to a deliberate plan to maintain the economic and political supremacy of certain groups who first colonized the American continent. The discussions, however, did not remain in the abstract, nor were the theories, as inaccurate as they were, limited to develop material of exclusively scientific debates. It quickly moved to practical applications with conclusions being drawn. *Undesirable* immigration was analyzed from all points of view: biological, anthropological, ethnographic, hereditary, from that of individual or collective psychology, of dominant ideas and prejudices, of customs and social and family relationships both in the countries of origin as well as in the land of adoption. However, the research was done with such monumental ignorance and bad faith that to read over time what was written during that period is beyond belief. One is stunned to discover how distinguished people, from whom one would expect balanced judgment and a fair-minded interpretation, let themselves get carried away out of stubbornness, by a preconceived thesis, and by racial antipathy to the point of blending in with the chorus of professional propagandists and mercenaries of anti-foreigner hatred. Government officials, university professors, men at the height of the most important professions plunged themselves into the shameful contest of baseless assertions, arbitrary conclusions, distortion of facts, and systematic slurs. All this in order to come to the conclusion that the chosen Nordic race, which had been able to ensure itself a high quality of life and to create political and social institutions that were superior to those of any other nation, was threatened at its core and in those characteristics that best distinguished it by the primitive hordes of southern and eastern Europe who had a very low quality of life and who were used to tremble under the scourge of tyrannies.

Limiting ourselves to what interests our present discussion, not only were the failings and shortcomings of our immigrants exaggerated and scrutinized through magnified lenses but also their virtues were interpreted as vices or antisocial qualities and twisted to demonstrate their mental and ethical inferiority. The spirit of attachment to the family was contrary to modern social tendencies that aimed to extend the scope of the individual, overcoming the familial grouping that retains the closed characteristics of the primitive human communities. In order to be good Americans, it is necessary for family ties to become much looser or even for the nucleus of immigrant families to break up. Worse still was when it was about the strong feeling of affection that the Italian immigrant had for his country and race. This was seen as the continuation of the spirit of the *clan* which, in a modern society, constitutes a danger and a very serious spiritual deficiency. Didn't the immigrant send money to his family who remained in Italy? He represented a liability and he undermined the economic sources of the country. With extraordinary bad faith, the Americans forgot that in order for the immigrant to earn ten he had to produce one hundred, and of those he was at least free to use as he wanted. Wasn't it at the forefront of the Italian immigrant's aspirations to return definitively to Italy after scraping together a fair bit of money? This meant that he did not feel attached to the country and could not be counted on as an essential and permanent component. And even here one has forgotten, whether it be through bad faith or lack of powers of observation, that the Italian immigrant regarded the years of his permanence in America as a type of sentence of hard labor, a period of hell during which he was aided by the sole idea to be one day economically independent. Whose fault was it if the immigrant was subjected to the harshest jobs, exposed to all sorts of abuse, and without any protection? Whose fault was it if the American production system of those times, for the categories of labor in which the unions had not yet established themselves, a working day of 12 hours was enforced? Whose fault was it if after 12 hours of shattering the toughest fibers of his body, the poor immigrant had to go close himself up in a hole without air and light and collapse, only to start again the next morning? Only one thing would have been surprising: if the immigrant worker were to become fond of a country in which his life was a torment and counted less than a dog's.

He tried to save in order not to be a burden on anyone, not even on public assistance. With his *hoarding*—it was said—he kept money from circulating. This was a capital offense. It was a period steeped in Manchester economics in which the immaturity and recklessness of a new and infantile people, both in thought and in values, believed to have discovered a perpetual land of plenty. There was a dance of mad confusion to the tune of dollars and the United States gave the impression of being a huge fair where everyone trained in offhand tricks, haranguing the cultured audience from a charlatan's booth, putting on spectacular representations, boasting of the virtues of the latest financial whim or of the most recent bond issued by the stock market, which was all the same, in order to have as much money as possible pass from another's pocket to one's own pocket. The harsh awakening occurred in 1929 when the system collapsed with the crash of a terrestrial catastrophe that swallowed like magic the economic amusement park with its colored balloons and phantasmagoric scenery. However, as long as the system lasted, it was sustained by the fundamental principle of continual circulation of money. Halting it or obstructing it in any way meant trouble! Anyone who was found guilty of this was considered a public enemy. You needed to spend all the money you earned, and the Americans, during those times, were obsessed by a real frenzy to spend as if money was burning holes in their pockets. It was common to find an American who, carrying a large wad of bills that he cleverly unfolded in view of everyone each time he pulled it out of his pocket, entered into *bars* and in other public places and would pay for all the patrons even if he had never seen them before. After spending every last dollar, he left calm, satisfied, and content as if he had completed a commendable action. The frugality of the Italians, who were taught over the centuries to plan for the future and guard against the ungrateful surprises that poured unexpectedly onto the heads of mortals, was considered just short of a crime. In other words, the lack of foresight of the savage was held in higher regard than one of the greatest powers bestowed to a civilized man: that of foresight and protection against uncertainty and the unknown. As long as this way of thinking was restricted to the ordinary citizens, deplorable as it may be, it could not do a great deal of harm. The biggest misfortune was that many of America's most distinguished figures in economic and social sciences took part in this exercise. With regard to this issue, let's remember one example that best illustrates the saying "the sting is in the tail" and the lack of equanimity with which the phenomenon of Italian migration is studied. In one of his studies, a man by the name of Henry Fairchild, a pillar of racist pseudoscience in the United

States, treats undesirable immigration.[17] At a certain point, he brings up the statistic of those admitted in institutions for the poor, elderly, and debilitated. With much surprise to the reader of the superior race (and it must have been an unexpected surprise for the professor as well), at the head of the statistics were those of Nordic origin. At the bottom were the undesirables, including the Italians whose percentages were among the lowest. The professor, much to his dismay, cannot go against the statistics. He explains them: one cannot deny that the immigrant groups of southern Europe have attained a greater degree of economic independence and have a greater sense of caution. However, *in cauda venenum*: the good professor adds his venomous jab. *Yes*, the Mediterranean people have attained those things through *a low standard of living*. So, an Irishman and a German, who are at the top of the statistics and have ended up in a poorhouse because they spent all that they earned, are more worthy of consideration than an Italian who has remained at home and stays within his means. This is without considering that a high standard of living often boils down to a high level of *whiskey*. One can find numerous examples of similar distortions of reasoning dictated by pure and simple malice. Some would be extremely comical if they did not arouse indignation in a little volume on our immigration compiled by a follower of the above mentioned professor whose guidelines and ideas were the source of inspiration. Unfortunately, the professor's disciple is of Italian origin.

In this little volume, the author tells us why Italian children's legs twist so easily. And you know why? Because their parents are anxious to see them walk early. This minion of a distinguished figure repeats a popular prejudice. No longer is it a question of a bad diet, lack of calcium in the bones, or a vitamin deficiency. No, it is a result of over-ambitious parents. The Italians, moreover, prefer fresh food to canned foods! How dreadful! And it's not because fresh foods are better for you than canned food, nor because from the latter there is the fear of food poisoning! Oh, no! It is only an aversion derived from the fact that in Italy, unlike in America, there are no adequate facilities to store food that easily spoils. Have you gotten the idea? We could

---

17   Henry Fairchild (1880-1956), a professor of sociology at New York University, was the author of the book *The Melting Pot Mistake* in 1926.

continue with more examples, and they would be quite amusing. We paused to talk about them only to give an idea of the levity, ignorance, animosity, and prejudice with which the Italian problem on American soil has been examined. Didn't the Italians rebel against the atrocious working conditions to which they were subjected in some places? Well, they were anarchists against whom the government was wise to take precautions. Didn't the Italians allow themselves to be easily convinced how to vote by the political *bosses*? It was a wrongdoing dependent in part on the lack of knowledge in a new country, and in part on the failure to understand what they wanted from them.

It was a wrongdoing whose cause is attributed principally to the American political system, with its *machines*, its *bosses*, and its *division leaders* whose power and bullying could not be avoided by our poor worker. However, it was not explained in this way. The Italians were people who, for centuries, were used to serve and obey passively. Therefore, they were *easily driven* forward like a herd of sheep by anyone who was shrewd and arrogant enough to put his stamp on them. As a result, they represented a danger for a country where freedom of choice and personal independence had always prevailed, where political coercions were not allowed, where delegates were nominated by way of public interest etc., etc. And, as you well know, they were born under a monarchy. *Kings, you know.* How could these people foster free thought if they had to obey a *King*? However, excluded among these *Kings* were those from England. That was something else, they tried to explain. It doesn't matter that the thirteen original states had to endure a war against it. Only the Irish resented the King of England. From this it is clear that even the anti-monarchy sentiment is not sincere but only serves as a pretext to attack the hated southern European immigration. And they paraded the usual *clichés* concerning American ideals that the recent immigrants were unable to understand. Freedom, for example. How could one of the recent arrivals from backward countries absorb the spirit of freedom that exists in America and breathe with the first cry of those who are fortunate to be born in this land? It is now important to open a parenthesis to explain what American freedom is all about.

It is one of the most colossal *bluffs* that a new people staged in order to devise a superiority over older nations who have gone through long and hard trials of historical experience. The confusion concerning the question of freedom is enormous and is largely wanted because no one can figure it out. The idea of freedom is confused with that of state and local autonomy. The United States is a free country because there is no centralized government; rather, there are as many governments as there are states. However, no one stops to consider the fact that each of these states can, in its own way, tyrannize the population with antiquated, dogmatic, and bizarre laws. Those least able to judge it are the foreign nations for whom the government of the United States is federal. It appears fantastically liberal because quite simply.... it doesn't govern. It gives this task to the states. These latter are dominated by the so-called political *machines* which, in turn, are totally at the service of capitalist interests. And here we return to the repeatedly debated question if a free regime is possible when the majority of the population is at the mercy of a few who can shape it as they choose with the threat of deprivation. And this is what exists in America. In the capitalist country par excellence, the large financial and productive organizations exercise on the life of the nation a power that is much more complete, rigid, and implacable than what exists in Europe, where capitalism has never had such a huge and unrestricted development. Oftentimes, the states are solely fiefdoms dependent upon some large individual or collective baronies: the Mellons in Pennsylvania, the Du Ponts in Delaware, the Anacondas, the copper mining company, in Montana. The examples can be multiplied for almost all the states of the Union. Lacking a strong central government that checks and limits absolute authority, the real government belongs to them. It is the large financial interests that tell the state governments and local administrations what they must and must not do. They place their trusted men in posts that represent the keystone of the entire economic mechanism of the country. They are the ones who ask for and obtain for their businesses a privileged legislation that transforms them into real monopolies. They are the ones who control the state legislatures, the courts, the city police, the militias of the various states, and the administrations of the large cities. The public utility companies are all-powerful and decide without any chance of opposition how the public should be treated. They make their influence felt in all branches of judicial, moral, civic, and social life. It is an influence that at times is subtle to the point of not being easily visible; however, it is no less powerful. Things appear before your eyes from time to time that are not possible to explain with the usual determinants. Some hidden influence must be at play. In recent years, there have been a number of cases of death sentences of people who were found guilty of crimes committed in order to claim a life insurance policy. To those who are familiar with the American justice system and the leniency with which atrocious crimes committed by very dangerous professional criminals are treated, some of these sentences have immediately appeared exaggerated and unjustified. The reason was hinted at by a few newspapers: very powerful insurance companies wanted an example. Juries and judges were quick to obey. The news was immediately retracted by those interested, but one knows how much certain retractions are worth. In America, this substitution of groups in the issuing of directives for dispositions of will, which should be the prerogative of central government on matters that regulate morality, customs, and economic relations of the various categories of citizens, is the rule. Such groups are composed of so-called pillars of society who decide in each community if someone who has come from other places can remain amongst them. In the event he arouses suspicion regarding the questionable orthodoxy of his principles or his conduct does not fully satisfy the Elders of Zion, it is made clear to him to vacate within a definite time. In the event he does not obey, an angered crowd will forcibly drag him to the borders of the jurisdiction not without duly beating and humiliating him. The procedure is considered perfectly normal. It is these same Elders of Zion who pit the community against strikers and organize the lynchings. There are large companies, such as those in mining, that employ their own militiamen, equipped with rifles, machine guns, poison gas, and pineapple bombs: perfect combat gear. The treatment that the workers receive from the thugs recruited among the most ferocious gangs of the seediest slums cannot even be compared to Czarist Russia. The famous *iron and coal police* of the coal mine barons of Pennsylvania is known throughout the world for its bloody brutality in its clamp-down of strikes. Even public service companies that operate in the cities, such as that of the New York subway system, have their own special police whose abuse of peaceful citizens causes scandals and very lively protests. A great fuss is made in the newspapers, then everything returns to silence. And the private police remain.

When you happen to talk with an American about such systems in a country of so-called freedom, he, besides not being excessively outraged as occurs with Europeans, will respond that everyone has the right to express his own opinions through the election ballot and that, moreover, can have his voice heard at meetings or can spread his ideas through the press. Doesn't freedom of speech and press exist in America? That'll be the day! The biggest hoax is the clamor surrounding elections when people fool themselves into believing for a moment that they rule. Go for a moment and stand up against an influential political machine and you will see what happens. The *gangs* in power will take all measures to keep the opposing masses from the voting booths, including physical violence. In the best case scenario, the famous freedom to choose representatives consists of giving your vote to one of the ruling *gangs*. And your vote will count as much as can be expected, that is less than nothing if cast against the major competing interests. The same can be said for freedom of the press. Your protest will end up among the letters from the public. However, if you allow yourself to go too far to the bottom of things and direct your attacks at the invisible government controlled by capitalism, your letter will not be published. It's because the press is an integral part of the system. The only consolation you will have is to vent by sending your thoughts to some weekly magazine or newspaper that publishes a few thousand copies no one reads.

We have extended our discussion on this topic to explain the type of ideals that undesirable immigration could not penetrate. And with good reason. Coming from countries where there is more order, it was not possible to penetrate the chaos. The truth is that the American people are considered *res nullius* by the invisible power that governs them and uses them exclusively as an instrument to make money. Capitalism dominates them, it divests them, and it controls with an iron fist even their slightest actions, from the time they get up to the time they leave the movie theater and go to bed. You only have to look at the control the Ford Company wields over the life of its workers, or to be aware of the way with which the industrialists have neatly evaded the measures of the "new deal" by increasing salaries a few dollars and by expecting twice as much production from an overwhelmed and wearied work force, to understand the tyranny that weighs on the American people and makes every celebration of that alleged and exaggerated freedom appear ironic. Except that it is done with such artful subtlety that the famous sovereign people do not realize it. The American is left with the illusion that everything moves thanks to his work. He is occasionally fleeced of his savings and handed a ballot form, his skull is cracked by a club if he protests, and he is led to believe that he is free to speak, write, and yell all he wants. He is juggled between the baton of the police and the terror of *gangsters* without protection from either one, while being told that his extensive rights will always be respected. His life is regulated as if he is in prison, yet he is led to believe that there are no freer people in the world. And by hearing it constantly repeated, he ends up believing it. An American may even praise the political systems of other European nations and recognize the good that they have done for their people. However, he will unfailingly add with a sense of ill-concealed pride: yes, this is good for the Europeans, but we could never accept a similar system. On the basis of this conclusion, the Americans can accept being tyrannized by the lowest dregs of humanity with their *rackets* that impose a quota on food and businesses, they can remain under the threat of seeing someone dear to them kidnapped, they can tolerate being insulted by drunken and uncivil policemen, they can put up with criminal politicians and corrupt judges, and they can accept that their life is strictly controlled by a hidden power. However, they cannot admit to being governed honestly by a system based on ethical foundations that administers impartially the relations between the various social classes.

* * *

There is a deliberate attempt to create a misconception when comparing the political system of the United States with that of those nations whence the immigrants come so that the superiority of the first will emerge. The misconception was created by those who were in the know and who had definite aims to achieve through such propaganda. But a large number of Americans, in their colossal naiveté and ignorance, were truly convinced that the Europeans came to America to escape from the greedy tyranny of their countries. The same thing was done when discussing the economy. The authors who were committed to the anti-immigration campaign did not overlook any subject that would validate their thesis. They took the trouble to consult renowned studies on the conditions of the southern and island populations of Italy, like that of Franchetti and Sonnino,[18] old parliamentary debates and speeches in order to conclude: "so, you see! It can be drawn from their own words that these people who flood into our land lived in caves, and as far as their living standard, it is not much higher than that of an African savage." For those times and for the populations of certain Italian regions where there was no development, that could have also been true. It is just that the Americans were less entitled than others to criticize us because they had their own South, a South even more bleak and in a greater state of squalor and deterioration than ours. Even if the poverty amid the southern Italians was at times horrendous, they did not have the *white trash* or *white crackers*, as they were called. They didn't have the *clay eaters*, nor large sections of the population whose components were ravaged and stultified by the degrading poverty, by the diseases, and by the very serious mental defects that made them, and still make them, sure candidates for mental institutions, prisons, and poorhouses. And this is not in a poor country like ours but in a very rich land where something so shameful should in no way be tolerated. So much for superiority of race! The *poor whites* of the South, the degenerate groups of which we speak, belong without exception to the superior race, the Nordic blond and of Anglo-Saxon origin. Their purity has not been contaminated by subsequent arrivals due to the isolation in which they have remained for two or three centuries. The

18   In 1876 two members of the Italian Parliament, Leopoldo Franchetti (1847-1917) and Sidney Sonnino (1847-1922), presented to Parliament the first documented investigation on the social and economic conditions of Sicily in the post-Unification period, *La Sicilia nel 1876* (Florence: Tipografia di G. Barbera, 1877).

effects of having remained immune from heterogeneous blood lines have been disastrous. Nature's great experimental laboratory, not being influenced by brilliant theories, has shown that the superior human qualities, instead of perfecting and enhancing themselves due to the lack of mixing different ethnicities in order to produce a superman, are damaged, ruined, and deteriorated.

* * *

Freed from the superstructure of insubstantial theories, fanatical praise, rancorous polemics, and the falsification of facts and declarations, the history of populating the American continent appears to hinge on slave labor. Slavery, along with its methods and philosophy, has permeated the spirit of the American capitalist, industrial, and political classes. During its origins when the country had a great need for manpower, "negroes" were transported by force. Since the European conscience had rebelled against this inhuman practice, England decided to hunt down the slave ships and the shameful trade had to end. The "negroes" remained linked to the plantations of the southern states where they were bought and sold like livestock. They were freed, but not entirely, from the plantations by the Civil War. However, for the development of the New World, it was necessary to find human flesh elsewhere. America turned to the Chinese "*coolies.*" But these "*coolies*" immediately raised great concerns due to their being content with incredibly low living standards and their rapid increase in numbers. The first indication of displacement of the masses from southern Europe made one think of a new enormous reserve of human goods. The first small wave represented a liberation from the Asian threat. It was deemed that the "*coolies*" were expendable. Initially the immigration of Chinese women was prohibited, and the poor "yellow" men who had already settled on American soil found themselves in an unnatural situation as a result of being barred from any relationship with white women. Subsequently, the Asian immigration was prohibited altogether and the Chinese arriving from across the Pacific were cut off, like an amputated limb, from any ties and further relations with their relatives who remained in the homeland. These were distinctive slavery-like practices. The "negroes" were brought to the slave markets, sold at auctions and sent in distant places without considering whether they left loved ones behind: parents, wives, children whose hearts bled. The same trick was repeated with European immigration. When it was thought that this practice had become dangerous and cumbersome and the decision was made that America was saturated with them, it was abruptly cut off with the stroke of a sword, not caring that they were dealing with a live organism whose stumps were spilling blood. The eminently slavery-like system of quotas was then established. These people were nothing more than a number. No consideration at all was given if this strict and heartless number separated families, cut off affections, and placed people with close blood ties in the situation of never seeing one another again. The practice of the auction block where slaves were sold continued. However, one door remained open. The legislators had had the immeasurable generosity of not including in the quotas the other nations of the American continent whose immigration remained open. During the war, the influx of European immigrants ended spontaneously. There was a great need of labor due to the industrial pace that had accelerated to the maximum of its power. A large number of Mexicans and residents from the West Indies flocked to the United States, replacing the abandoned immigration from beyond the Atlantic. During the period of prosperity, they were allowed to remain. However, no sooner did this prosperity begin to decline, the same thing that happened to the Chinese and southern European immigration was repeated, except under a different form. The poor Mexicans and other immigrants from Central America were harassed in every way, sent away forcefully by the places where they had settled for years, and were required to reach as quickly as possible the border loading them on trains, trucks, and automobiles. Without suitable means, they needed to leave on foot. The important thing was that they vacate. Many children were born and raised on American soil. They were allowed to stay, but how could their parents leave them alone? The slavery-like procedure continued. And it continues in the requirements that regulate the admission of ridiculous quotas in which entry is still theoretically allowed. No moral humiliation or physical disgrace is spared to those who want to come to America. They are measured, examined, and probed. Additionally, anthropometric data and finger prints are taken, and they are classified according to the ethnic group they belong, just like a horse that goes to a show with its registered *pedigree* and how they used to do with the slaves who were displayed for the auction sale. All this without counting the endless, shameful, mortifying, and maddening interrogations done with the insulting crudeness of a small-time American official. It was as if everyone who was about to cross the threshold of the new land was a future criminal. The most tragic and painful part of the new policy toward foreigners, which has been enforced for some time, are the deportations. We are not talking about the justifiable deportations. We are talking about those done in order to persecute them or simply drive them out. Deportation is the Sword of Damocles that currently hangs over every immigrant who has not yet renounced his citizenship. It is a perennial threat against those who rebel against the unfair labor conditions that are prevalent in some regions. In other cases, deportation, besides being absurd, is a cruelty without equal. We'll give an example that can apply to all. Many children of immigrants are brought here at a very young age, when they are just a few months or a few years old. They have grown up in America and consider it their only home: they have no recollection of their place of origin. Despite considering themselves Americans and nothing but Americans, they are not, however, in fact. If their parents at the time of their birth were not American citizens, the children were considered by law to be foreigners. Many of these poor souls are unaware of this and did not think of obtaining citizenship papers. How could they have thought of it? In their very first childhood impressions, they can only recall America and American surroundings. For the life they lead and the environment in which they grow up, it is easy to run into trouble with the justice system. Sometimes they are minor offenses, but the immigration authorities take advantage of them to deport them. So that this is possible, their stay must be less than five years. Each trip abroad interrupts the foreigner's continuity of residence and he is considered a new arrival. On the basis of this regulation, the *detectives* charged to investigate the status of the individual under review resort to a thousand small tricks to trap him in order to prove his deportability.

"Have you been to Canada?," they ask.

Who hasn't taken a trip to Canada, which is like an appendage to the United States? The poor fellow under interrogation responds naively yes. He's ruined. This confession is enough to interrupt continued residency and make him subject to deportation. Now, imagine what must be the condition of an individual who, even if guilty of some offense, sees himself condemned to a perpetual exile in a country that is foreign to him, whose language he does not speak, where he has no friends or relatives, nor the possibility to easily adapt to new ways of life, much less earn a living.

The closing of immigration was a serious blow to the Italian communities in America. Those types of businesses based exclusively on the immigration flow and those in wholesale and retail trade based on an Italian clientele were the first to suffer. The volume of trade began gradually to wane until it became, in a number of cases, insignificant. Private banks, shipping offices, import stores, *groceries*, but especially articles of consumption that they were accustomed to in Italy—restaurants, cafes, hotels, haberdasheries—were maintained out of desperation by the owners who were terrorized by the thought of ending up in the streets rather than for reasons that would justify their existence. After having agonized at length, one after the other began to close by the hundreds. The tragedy of small trade in the Italian neighborhoods was so sad that it broke your heart. It will continue until the trajectory of what were Italian activities in America, dedicated exclusively to satisfy the needs of the Italians, will have been completed. Many cities once inhabited by our countrymen were depopulated: the joyful bustle gave way to silence and gloom, and the remaining sparse population has the look and attitude of survivors of a catastrophe. Some social groups, particularly professionals, have suffered immensely by the stoppage of immigration. Physicians, pharmacists, and lawyers have seen their clients, who were a source of subsistence, dissipate. As a result of the extreme mobility of its population, there has never been a stable clientele in America. However, in the past, when immigration was in full force, the losses due to relocation were offset by the addition of recently arrived immigrants. For some time, there have been no new arrivals. Those professionals who did not think about it, or were not in any condition of setting something aside for a rainy day, were left in bad financial shape in their declining years. Many ended badly: a gun shot put an end to their anguish. If the Italian communities in America have suffered considerable economic damages, as a result of the closing of immigration, the moral damages have been incalculable. The commonality of thought, customs, and affections that joined the expatriates to the vast majority of the Italian people has been severed. Ideas, passions, friendships, family relationships, knowledge of public events, stories of private experiences and also whispers of gossip were kept alive by this ongoing ebb and flow of people who, by way of the ocean, came and went from countries of origin with such a frequency that the immigrant could know day by day all that was happening in his country or in his hometown. There was always his friend so and so who arrived or another friend who left. It was if a human bridge laid over the Atlantic would keep the Italian offshoot in America alive and joined to the main trunk. With the closing of immigration, the ties have dried up to the point of withering completely. The news became much less frequent and the immigrants began to focus all their attention and activities on local things. Resigned by then to remain detached from their ethnic origins, they made a virtue of necessity. They decided to transform themselves into Americans as soon as possible. They asked for and obtained citizenship and became increasingly less interested in what took place on the other side of the Atlantic. Their children almost never heard anymore Italian spoken in the home: friends and relatives from Italy, with whom they were forced to use their mother tongue, no longer arrived. The separation had occurred: the legions of Italians who began to pour onto the shores of the United States more than fifty years ago, those strange droves of immigrants who concerned the Americans, will be incorporated into the American population in a not too distant future and will be an integral part of it. The original imprint will be completely canceled.

IX. THE HOUR OF THE ITALIANS

The admiration that the Americans had for the Italian immigrants and for the Italians in Italy in the pre-war and immediate post war years was by no means excessive. The Americans were divided into two categories: the almost totality of those who never stepped foot outside of the United States and, in many cases, had never crossed the boundaries of their own state; and the very few who traveled and had seen various European countries, including Italy. The first group judged us on the basis of the human masses that spewed out daily from the ocean liners. From what has been previously discussed, their opinion could not be too flattering. As for the second group, when they wanted to be kind, they spoke of Venice, the Grand Canal, the pigeons of Saint Mark's Square, the Leaning Tower of Pisa, Saint Peter's, the Vatican, the Swiss Guards, and Vesuvius. The Italian landscape was so romantic! Only in Italy could one experience certain *thrills*: one could expect at any time to see pop out of some ruin a bandit with a feather in his cap and gun aimed. And how can you express in words the Colosseum under a full moon! And what a bunch of thieves, those hotel owners, those carriage drivers, those guides, and those shopkeepers! They rip you off with such skill that you don't even realize it. It was dangerous, however, for a woman to venture out on the main streets without an escort. Oh, the beauty of those columns, those arches, those old moss-covered stones. And the churches! The Florence Cathedral, Santa Maria Novella, Monreale, the catacombs! Paintings and statues that induced in their mind an indescribable confusion. But nothing about modern Italy, except insults: our dirty cities with Naples in the lead, the homeless beggars lying in the sun, women were removing lice in full view of everyone, petulant *scugnizzi*, disgusting beggars from whom it was impossible to get away and who stuck their horrible stumps in your face. Widespread corruption and an air of poverty and decadence everywhere. These were, more or less, the general impressions of the travelers. The school books did the rest. The frivolousness and scornful condescension with which they spoke about us was revolting. In the school texts, Italy was described as a land with volcanoes that always erupted. Its inhabitants, on par with the natives of Africa and Oceania, had strange customs and ate macaroni with their hands. The Italians were an emotional people and, therefore, they had some good painters, sculptors, and musicians. In the pictures, one found groups of women sitting on steps in steep, narrow alleys, fishermen and longboats, stalls of Neapolitan street vendors and painted Sicilian carts. If they referenced our history, it was a mess. The unification of Italy was the work of the French and English. Italy had the awful idea of going to tease the Africans and had suffered a terrible defeat at Adua. They deserved it! Worst yet was when they began to discuss our war. Because don't think that the Great War raised one iota the Americans' esteem of us. Just like our colonial history was compressed into Adua, our epic endeavor during the great conflagration was summed up in Caporetto. The defeats sustained by the Allies on the other fronts did not count: they are inevitable and also glorious. The only truly great defeat of the entire war was that of Caporetto. If there is a country where our war has been disregarded and mistreated in the most shameful of ways, where our contribution to the cause of the Allies has been distorted to the point of being inconsequential or completely ignored, that country is America. Suffice it to say that more attention has been accorded to the war efforts of the Serbs than to ours. And let's not mention the exaggerated assessment of American aid to the Allies. Here one touches on the absurd. In the apportionment of wartime distinctions of the respective nations during the Great War, the 50,000 American casualties on French soil have greater weight than our 600,000 dead on the Carso front. That the war did not contribute to our gaining an inch in the Americans' esteem can be shown by the fact that in the 1921 restrictive law of immigration (the one before the latest and that was designed on the basis of strictly racist criteria), greater room was made for the Germans, yesterday's enemies, than for the Italian allies.

The Americans' attention to our situation and the incentive to study it seriously was encouraged by the rise of fascism. After some initial resistance, early misunderstandings, and first hostilities, a more measured and fair-minded attitude began to form that allowed for a more objective examination of what took place on the other side of the Atlantic. At the beginning, there were many uncertainties and no one dared to venture a candid and explicit opinion. It was said that the experiment would not last more than six months and would end in a disaster. A disaster was created, and a tremendous one, in the United States while the Italian *esperimento* proceeded triumphantly. It did not last the six months predicted, rather six years and then six more years. Moreover, all signs indicated that this figure would double and multiply for an undefined period of time and would assume the proportions and grandeur of an epoch. However, there were other things just short of a miracle that materialized. In the richest country in the world, there appeared endless *bread lines* for the impoverished who waited hours in extreme weather conditions for a bowl of soup and a piece of bread. The public parks, open courtyards, the entryways of tenement buildings, and the stairwells of the *subways* were literally covered with people sleeping who wrapped themselves in newspapers to fend off the cold. They were the unsheltered homeless who, chased away by the police, moved continuously from one place to another in the hope of being able to sleep a few hours on the naked earth. And so, in a country poor in natural resources and about which the Americans did not speak without a smirk of pity or an air of condescending superiority, these things did not occur. Everyone had bread and a roof over his head, if not an automobile and a radio, nor did you see disheartening scenes, which were so common in America, of families with a flock of children thrown out into the street with very few furnishings because of their failure to pay rent. At least something had to be good in the Italian social and political structure. An interest in the corporative system developed in America. They asked for information and explanations about the idea that shaped it and how it worked. Why couldn't something similar be applied in America and put an end to the old cannibalistic individualism? The press spread the news of the formidable Italian renewal, and brief glimpses of this were seen on the movie screen: majestic streets, gigantic bridges, the draining of the swamps, and the founding of new cities. It was no longer a case of *dolce far niente*, the stereotypical phrase dear to every scribbler who would babble about our ways. It was an entire people devoted to the hard and joyful effort of making the country more powerful, greater, and more respected. The preconceived ideas of Italian indolence,

Italian lethargy, and Italian laziness began to dissolve. An interest in Italy intensified to the point of motivating many of them to cross the ocean and see for themselves all that was happening on the other side. And they found cities modernized, ordered, and clean, much cleaner than American cities, without *scugnizzi*, without beggars, without the homeless lying in the sun, and without groups of loafers standing on street corners, a most common sight in the American urban centers. Public safety was excellent and there was no fear of armed robberies or abductions. Children were well taken care of and child care was guaranteed. The amazed travelers wrote about these things in private letters to friends and relatives and published their impressions in newspapers and magazines.

Even the press, which was usually skeptical when it came to Italy, had a change of mind. But more than the halting, measured, and whispered recognition of the bodies of public opinion, individual recognition is of greater worth when it is expressed spontaneously and directly by Americans who earn their living through hard work. They know how difficult it is to make a living for oneself and for a family under the current conditions in America, and how precarious and uncertain their status is, and how the *common people* are perpetually at the mercy of a turbine that sweeps them, breaks them down, and disperses them like dried leaves.

"It's wonderful," they confess, that in a country without great resources people can earn a living and be sure to have at least a roof over their head. Credit needs to be given to *that man*. And when they say *that man*, they mean Mussolini. A strong personality always demands the attention of Americans to any race or creed it belongs. The giant figure of Mussolini that towers over the men of his era made a tremendous impression on their imagination. Also—and perhaps we should say above all—an impression was made on the imagination of those Americans who meddle very little in politics and have no interest whatsoever in social and economic theories. Their spirit is freer from preconceptions, their mind is not clouded by rigid ideological backgrounds, nor distorted by inflexible principles that are derived from past eras and no longer conform with present-day life. They are the ones who recognize spontaneously the greatness of a man who has snatched his country from chaos and kept its people from the precipice of ruin. It is they who have no taboos to observe, nor sacred demo-liberal fetishes to worship, who give credit, as they say, to a man who has given a new life to a people, restoring a respect and pride in themselves and regaining the respect and the esteem of the world. Still other miracles have occurred since the advent of fascism that have aroused the amazement of the Americans just like any unforeseeable and unimaginable thing. The Italians have become an athletic people. Those who are familiar with the integral part that sports play in American life can understand the importance of such a fact in the different opinion of our people. The Italian is no longer considered weak, faint hearted, clumsy, and awkward. His entrance on the scene has been most striking and dramatic. Some real giants of Italian stock have stood on the podium of one of the American sports that stirs the most partisan passion, praise, and enthusiasm: Firpo, Campolo, and Carnera.[19] The first two were born in a foreign land but this did not diminish the admiration for a race that could produce such behemoths.[20] With the world championship captured by Carnera, the short boxing career of the Italians in America reached its zenith. What was extraordinary about this was not in the pure and simple fact that one man defeated another man but rather in the way it happened. Anyone who would have ventured a guess twenty years ago that there would be an Italian boxing champion would have elicited roaring laughter and would have been considered a comedian. Boxing was a sport that was at that time totally in the hands of the Irish, and those who cautiously approached to claim some secondary role had to take an Irish name. The children of our immigrants, especially those who came from the working-class areas, were deeply mortified that they did not see an Italian name appear among the stars of the major American sports. They ended up considering it a congenital inferiority of the stock to which they belonged. They remained mortified because, as a

---

19   Luis Angel Firpo (1894-1950) and Victorio Campolo (1903-?) were both Argentine boxers of Italian descent. Primo Carnera (1906-1967), who was born in Sequals (then in the Province of Udine, now in the Province of Pordenone), was considered a national hero during fascism.

20   Records indicate that Victorio Campolo was born in Reggio Calabria, Italy.

result of their rudimentary education, it was the only thing they were able to appreciate. They couldn't certainly find any consolation in the brilliant successes of Italians in intellectual fields nor in the great past of their land of origin. In order to appreciate how their somber spirits were excited by this new feeling, one would only need to witness the intense interest that was spurred among the children of immigrants by the appearance of great champions with Italian names in the athletic arena. On the evening before a major decisive match, they would run around their neighborhoods waving the sports newspapers and getting into endless heated discussions on the talents of the various athletes and on the amazing punches that most impressed them. One would come across the names of Giorgetti,[21] Gene Sarazen,[22] Canzoneri,[23] Firpo, Campolo; above them all, there soared that of *Caanèra, Caanèra, Caanèra*, as they called him. They had never seen such splendor! They made up for the many years in which they were forced to pronounce only Irish, English, and German names.

Just a few years before the Italian athletes began to head toward America, the Italo-Americans had invaded those fields that, two or three decades earlier, the northern Europeans considered their exclusive dominion. At first, it seemed strange to find here and there some names in the minor sports and in the lighter weight classes of *boxing*. Slowly, Italian names—occasionally strange, long, and unpronounceable Italian names—began to multiply. In the world class sports of *golf*, auto racing, the six-day bicycle race and even *baseball* and *football*, in many cases the athletes of Italian descent won championships and many others came close to reaching similar heights and were recognized for their incomparable talent. In the Olympic Games of Los Angeles, our teams left the American spectators breathless on more than one occasion. And now there is no competition of a certain importance in any sport, both in the eastern, western, or southern parts of the United States, in which the competing teams, both professional, college, or any other

---

21   Franco Giorgetti (1902-1983) was an Italian racing cyclist and Olympic gold medalist.

22   Eugenio (Gene) Sarazen (1902-1999) was a professional golfer whose parents were Sicilian immigrants.

23   Tony Cazoneri (1908-1959) was a professional boxer.

level, do not include Italian athletes whose names suddenly jump right out at you in the newspapers' headlines shocking its readers.

And the great ocean liners landed on the American shores. Those new, enormous luxury liners were the preferred means of travel for political and economic leaders as well as celebrities of all kinds. Crowds of thousands, composed of all types of people, visited them in long, enthusiastic lines, and large groups remained permanently on the docks, as if to set up a watchful guard. We have come a long way from the heaps of human cargo that were transported during the great migration in which the steerage holds of the ships were stacked with the poor souls who were forced to abandon their native land. The newspapers described the ship's structure, its comforts for every class of traveler, spacious lounges, artistic décor, and health and sanitary provisions. In their descriptions and illustrations, they compared the enormous size of the huge steamships with their most imposing *skyscrapers*, which were not much higher. As a result, the general public realized that the inventiveness, skill, staff excellence, and other talents required to build a large ocean liner were no less than those necessary to build those titans of modern construction that bestowed upon the greatest city in the world the characteristic skyline of which it is so proud. As if to seal the image of grandeur and splendor that the enchanting buildings from Italian shores had provoked in the crowds, the largest of them, the *Rex*, won the coveted *nastro azzurro* award for crossing the Atlantic in the fastest time.[24] This event was also highly publicized by the newspapers and resonated in the minds of Americans who are never indifferent when it comes to *records* of any kind that have been broken or are to be broken.

The transatlantic flight of General Balbo caused an indescribable buzz of expectation and enthusiasm.[25] Hundreds of thousands of people, and we are not alluding exclusively to our fellow Italians, waited for hours and hours along the route where the squadron of planes were

---

24   In 1933 the ocean liner SS Rex won the coveted *Nastro Azzuro* ("Blue Riband") race across the Atlantic.

25   Italo Balbo (1896-1940) was an Italian fascist leader and Italy's Marshal of the Air Force, who led an Italian air armada in a transatlantic flight to the 1933 Chicago World's Fair.

to pass. And when the great feat obtained its awe-inspiring result, it seemed to mark a new historical epoch. American aviators had accomplished in this field outstanding individual achievements: the names of Lindbergh and Amelia Earhart will forever remain etched in the history of human conquests over the blind hostilities of nature. However, in the era that it was accomplished, no one had ever seen, nor had the most audacious imagination ever dreamed, that a squadron of air machines would be capable of flying over the ocean in perfect formation as if it had executed a maneuver on an aviation field.

* * *

On the basis of what we have discussed, a conclusion becomes obvious: the figure of the Italian from the postwar period forward, and especially since the advent of fascism, has changed. One can see this in those who have arrived in America during this period for a temporary stay or to settle here permanently. They are no longer the Italians of the end of the last century with a sense of physical and moral inferiority that, after being impressed upon their personality from the days in their home country, was reaffirmed in all sorts of ways in their country of adoption. Gone is that air of submissiveness, that stooped and shuffling gait of beggars, that imploring expression in their eyes that was so painful to look at, like someone who was always expecting a blow from out of the blue. Nor does one find any longer the subdued attitude of someone who is used to being insulted, humiliated, abused and does not hope for better treatment. In the last two decades, the dazed and empty look caused by such a new and different environment, which made one think of a human being transported to another planet, is no longer common to those arriving in America. They arrived with their heads high with pride, ready to appreciate what was new and advanced but without any sense of undue humiliation toward the foreigner and without abject praise of others' unattainable superiority. This is also due to the fact that the distances between the Americans and us have been shortened. Before the war, the Italian cities, despite their centuries of fame and glory, could be considered large villages still immersed in the languid Middle Ages in light of the modern standards that were indispensable to the major urban centers. Communications were rudimentary, public services—telephones, aqueducts, sewers, schools, hospitals, ambulances, libraries, shelters for children and for the elderly—did not exist or their functionality was fifty years behind the more advanced countries. It was only natural that the immigrants at that time, even those arriving from cities, developed a perception of irreparable inferiority of their homeland. However, with the rhythm that Mussolini has given to national renewal, with the rapid, magnificent transformation of our cities, given the due proportion of the relative size, wealth, and abundance of natural resources and number of inhabitants of the two countries, Italy not only is not irreparably behind the United States but in many things, like social measures, has decidedly surpassed the United States. The Italians who have recently moved to America, besides not feeling overwhelmed by what they find, are able to compare, contrast, and form their own opinions of the relative merits of the technical systems and the American social and political organizations with those that exist in their homeland. What mainly discouraged the old Italian immigrants was the fact that they could not count on the aid and protection of their own country. The Italian representatives abroad had, in those times, the instructions to minimize as much as possible any nuisance to the government. And they rigorously complied. The immigrant of those times never gave any thought of asking the Italian officials for assistance even though it was their duty to guide him and support him. The immigrant felt alone and lost in a boundless sea of humanity. He had to rely solely on his own strengths. It is totally different for an Italian who now migrates to a new land. He knows he has behind him a powerful and great country that extends its protective hand to the most remote corners of the globe for its children. He knows that he can count on his country and that, when all is lost, he will always be able to escape back to his womb where he will be welcomed but not with the ironic disdain that once greeted the immigrant who had not made it rich. Instead, he will find there friendly hands that will steer him toward work and get him back in shape morally and physically from the misfortunes suffered elsewhere. The new figure of the Italian has not only changed in spirit but also has improved physically. He has gained a vigor and a physical presence that would have been impossible to find in those poor immigrants of earlier times. Upright, dynamic, bright-eyed, full of curiosity and a desire to learn, and determined not to be stepped on, the Italian who crosses the ocean is the living expression of the profound transformation that has occurred in his native country.

The Italian who goes abroad is no longer an immigrant but an expatriate. The importance that is owed to this change, planned personally by Mussolini, has not been accorded. It is not a formal change but a new status that reflects the great spiritual and political transformation of the Italian people as a result of the advent of the fascist regime. A stigma was attached to the definition of *emigrato* that needed to be erased. It summed up years of misery and humiliation and revived the idea of long caravans with bag over shoulder waiting along the docks of the ports of embarkation. It was the sad period of the renunciation of Egypt, of the *crumeri* of Tunis, of the massacre of Dogali,[26] and of the unfortunate battle of Adwa.[27] Those who expatriate today go abroad not to beg for bread or to subject themselves to "unskilled" jobs where they are badly paid and held in contempt by local workers. They go there to find a field suitable to their craft and their competency, a field that will lead to a worthwhile career, will prosper and do honor to their homeland. The Italian, in other words, has come of age. He has come of age in his country and he has done so in the communities of America. In spite of considerable shortcomings and serious deficiencies due primarily to being the last to arrive in a place where others have already secured the best jobs, both our compatriots who left their native land many years ago as well as their children born in their adopted land show each day that they know how to do it and that they can do it. The fact that the Americans have largely modified, or are gradually modifying, their prejudices concerning us can be seen in every situation of public and private life in the United States. Now, it is the spontaneous recognition of one of our good qualities and later it will be the fair acknowledgement of

26   The Battle of Dogali was fought in January 1887 between Italy and Ethiopia in Dogali, near Massawa in present day Eritrea.

27   The Battle of Adwa was a crushing defeat of an invading Italian army in March 1896 at the hands of Ethiopian forces.

our accomplishments in a variety of human activities. Other times, it will be the admiration for our intelligence, poise, seriousness, positive nature, and for an absence of hysterics and fanaticism. Undoubtedly, there are still stubborn hostilities. The old constituents who have the basic political and economic principles of American life in hand present a tremendous resistance to the penetration of newcomers who could upset the well-ordered social structure in which they have secured the best part. But time will bring justice to such unjustified aversions and the Italians will assume a place in American life that they deserve.

X. THE RETURN OF THE LOST CHILDREN

Our immigrants have not produced any cultural contribution in their country of adoption because they do not have any culture. Nor have they been able to hand down a culture to their children, a culture that, besides sinking its roots in the most remote origins of its people, differs from the dominant culture of a place and, in a certain way, completes it and complements it. They have not even been able to hand down to them the precious legacy of a pure language: only some crude dialects that the new generations refuse to speak from an early age, having recognized that it is a rough form of a language without any real importance as an instrument of communication. In very few homes of our immigrants has there existed a book shelf with Italian books. Even in the homes of professionals, it was rare to find, except for vocational texts that dated back to the years of graduation, books that revealed how one of the residents kept current with what people were thinking, writing, and discussing in Italy; in other words, that anyone was interested in the intellectual activity in the land of his birthplace. Everyone knows how important it is to have a small library in the home for the fulfillment of an intellectual education and for the formation of the character of the adolescents. We're not talking about school texts, which are not willingly opened, but books on various subjects that may attract the curiosity and imagination of young children in those moments when they feel drawn toward certain topics and more disposed toward acquiring from them an enduring impression. However, what would have happened here is, even if there were a library, the little Italo-Americans would not have been capable of making use of it because of their ignorance of the language due to the indifference of their parents in teaching it to them or to ensure that others could instruct them. In other words, in order for the Italians born on American soil to learn the culture of their fathers, at least in its basic and distinctive elements, two things were needed: that Italian was spoken in the families and that a certain intellectual atmosphere, combined with the frequent buying of new books, existed. It is a pity that this has not occurred. One truly regrets to see the facility with which some Italian children learn the language of their fathers, especially if one speaks Italian in the home. In the frenzy of daily worries, the parents have barely enough time to teach them the first part of the alphabet. The remainder of the time they do it on their own. You find some cases that appear miraculous. You ask a child who reads and understands Italian very well what school he attended.

"No school," is the reply, "I learned on my own. Daddy taught me how to read the letters of the Italian alphabet." The parents confirm this. It was enough for them to hear just a few times how the child put syllables together and what are the sounds of the vowels and consonants. This can be explained. Being a phonetic language, Italian is a walk in the park for those who are forced to study English, a language that is written in one way and spoken in another, and the sounds are not the same as the letters, whether they be a vowel or a consonant. They are pronounced in eight or ten different ways depending on their placement or on the origins of the word in which they are included. One of the longest and most complicated courses is the so-called *spelling* course. For us, this is limited to the first grade. Once you've learned it, that's it. As for English, you cannot escape *spelling* even in courses at the university. You cannot say you know a word unless, besides hearing it pronounced, you know letter by letter how it is written. From a thorny area that can never be walked on barefoot, the children of immigrants, when they turn to study Italian, find the task so simple that they proceed at such a fast pace to the point of arousing astonishment. It would not have taken much for the children of our people to learn the language of their ancestors and from this develop a culture that is not standardized like the one acquired in the American school system.

However, this did not happen. Ninety per cent of the immigrants did not speak Italian. In those same families in which the parents could have taught their children, they had too many financial worries, too many demands from the fierce struggle to survive, for them to focus seriously on the education of their children. The teaching of Italian seemed like an almost fruitless effort and an extravagance that would not have had much use in the practical world. It is right to recognize that much has been done in this area by parochial schools and by the initiative of an enlightened and enthusiastic small group of volunteers to teach Italian in American schools. But the serious wrong had already occurred and it would be difficult to repair it no matter how much effort is expended in the future. The most deplorable result of such a spiritual deficiency in the life of our people in America is that the children of immigrants—and we are talking about those who have benefited from an American education and have received a university degree—have a very confused and rudimentary idea of Italy's past. Nor do they have any idea of what Italy represents in the modern world. Even worse is when they learn in the American schools, both from the school books and from the mouth of a teacher, just a few and hasty notions in this regard with Italy's part in the history of humanity being systematically diminished, degraded, muted, altered, and distorted. Their culture is not adequate and independent enough to refute the false information that is conveyed, nor are they capable of forming more precise ideas regarding historical events, on the causes that produced them and the effects derived from them, and of the influence that the Italian civilization and culture has had on human progress. From what they say and on the basis of the immediate results, they acquire an inferiority complex that, being instilled in their minds with skill and diabolical persistence, will be inherent in their personality for the rest of their lives. They will fall in worship before everything American or what passes for American, and they consider everything that has not been produced under the shadow of the stars and stripes as totally inferior. The history of the world begins with the landing of the pilgrims at Plymouth Rock: before that there was only chaos, barbarism, darkness, crying, and the gnashing of teeth. The greatest men in the world have been Washington, Lincoln, Edison, and Ford. Franklin discovered electricity and the Americans have been involved directly or indirectly in all other discoveries. This sense of inferiority has never allowed the Italo-Americans up to now to adopt an independent attitude either in the political sphere or in the judicial, administrative, ethical, and technical sphere, and not even in a purely intellectual one. This is precisely what those groups who still have their hands on America's destiny counted on. To the children of the immigrants, it appears that, differentiating themselves so much from how a large bulk of the population thinks and acts or bringing an unusual perspective to this or that subject, they must not seem American enough. And both they and the descendants of any other ethnic group fear nothing more than the accusation of a non-genuine Americanism, an Americanism that is not one hundred per cent. They always see someone with a finger pointed at them accusing them of being *un-American*. Whether it be a result of the aforementioned absence of an authentic culture or of a scarcity of spirit that prevents them for having any trust in their own strengths, and above all because of the fear of being considered *aliens* in mind and spirit, they end up lining up behind the most discredited political *machines* with whom they come into contact and from whom they hope to be carried along, as long as they remain loyal and orderly. Never should there be an act of independence, never an act of rebellion, never an initiative that demonstrates they have a thought of their own to share or a greater awareness of what the duties of a citizen should be, and especially of a citizen who aspires towards a political office. And God knows there is a need in America for men who have different political and social ideas, men who make people understand the need to renew the fundamental institutions of the country. The American judicial system is a confused and tangled thicket of countless laws that overlap with each other, cancel each other out, need constant interpretations due to their lack of clarity, and are frequently inapplicable as a result of the flawed manner in which they have been thought through. The federal laws are in conflict with those of the states and both legislations interfere with the local communities. The so-called *common law*, passed on to America from England, is not based on peremptory and explicit laws, but is collected in a ponderous and unclear body of laws by which every judge rules in his own way and according to prevalent trends of public opinion in a certain moment, the social conditions, and the ties of family, friendship, and protection from which the person being judged benefits. What emerges are egregious verdicts as a result of their absurdity and injustice. The American citizen is never sure what he is allowed or not allowed to do. Perfectly innocent actions fall foul of some antiquated or badly interpreted law by the police and prosecutors, with the person who commits them being delivered a sentence that comes out of nowhere. On the other hand, someone who is guilty of serious crimes succeeds in many cases in getting away scot-free through procedural loopholes made possible by the flexibility of the law. One does not feel the need for a radical reform of the entire civil and criminal legislation of the United States because the American people lack a judicial sense. This is lacking because their original imprint was given to them by the Nordic people who never enjoyed a reputation of possessing such qualities to a superior degree. Moreover, the manner in which America was populated and colonized resulted in it not having a foundation of laws and rules. Everyone believes that so it must be and how things should go forward. In no other area as this is there a greater need for Roman balance, clarity, Roman vision, lucidity, Roman interpretation, Roman sculptural codification, and Roman righteousness of judgment. And who better than the children of our stock could have endowed America with these incomparable qualities? This is assuming that their spirit and their thought have been shaped by centuries of Italian culture. Even in the political arena, the contribution of a long, historical experience, of a greater independence of judgment and inspiration, would have been precious on the part of the descendants of a people gifted with genius and unlimited intellectual resources. The United States is faced daily with antiquated institutions that the original little 13 colonies established 150 years ago. These institutions prevent them from progressing and resolving the vital problems of present times. They are kept standing by the persistence and fanaticism of some traditionalist groups who fear a collapse as soon as they are subject to amendments. The American people are kept harnessed to them by the imposing capitalist interests that receive from the Constitution, intended to protect the privileged groups, a first encouragement and the original impulse to develop and expand. They stood before the children of our immigrants like an iron wall, the most formidable obstacle to their progress in an era in which everything there was to take in America had already been hoarded and monopolized by those who had come before them. They need to devote themselves to the task of destroying these laws and replace them with new ones that give everyone the opportunity to move forward and win stable and independent positions. They need to beat down all the old rubbish that has hindered American life, all the residue of medieval bigotry, of religious sectarianism, and of political intolerance of race and customs. And instead? They do not even realize the existence of such problems. They repeat the *cant* that has filled their minds at school: the American institutions are the best in the world and it is a crime to expect to change them. Those of other countries are tyrannical and backwards. Those who propose to introduce changes that do not correspond to the tradition that made America great are *un-American* and must be considered an enemy. And not one of the children of Italians (and this can also be said for all the recent immigrants with the exception perhaps of the Jews) stops for a moment and considers the enormity of such an idea, much less being predisposed to fight for it. With this in mind, quite a few of the most intelligent minds of our communities (and we are talking about those who originally came from Italy and have obtained American citizenship) asked themselves if it is worth getting all excited to nominate the descendants of Italians to public offices. What do these people have that is Italian except for their name? Do they have a patrimony of ideas that are their own, a program that distinguishes them and raises them above the stinking quagmire of *rabble* and its most typical exponents who get worked up in time for the elections? However, let's be clear on this point. We do not expect them to wave the Italian flag, which would not only make them look ridiculous but also disloyal to their country of birth. Nevertheless, it is revolting to see them accept all the views, the gestures, ways of thinking and expressing oneself of the half-wild, drunken Irish politicians who transplanted in America the procedures and mentality of the Green Erinyes *clans*. Because, unfortunately, the descendants of our immigrants, like the lowest form of American politicians, see problems exclusively from the point of view of the political *gangs* to which they belong, use the same vulgar and ludicrous words in order to connect with the crude and ignorant public, assume the same demagogic attitudes that make them the darlings of crowds, and resort like others to the exaggerated cries of barkers at a fair, of that great fair of irresponsibility that is American politics.

* * *

We spoke earlier of the tragic condition of Italo-Americans who feel rejected by seemingly invisible forces each time they attempt to penetrate, either for business reasons or to satisfy social aspirations, spheres of American society that, having been constituted for quite some time, claim the right to keep the new arrivals who are determined to climb the social ladder at a distance. Not being able to fall back into an Italian environment that they did not respect and where they felt very uneasy, they ended up remaining in a type of neutral zone in which they dealt with each other as well as socialized and married among themselves. However, with the arrival of fascism, a new phenomenon has occurred. Never before have so many Italo-Americans shown such an interest in the country of their fathers, its history, its customs, and in the extraordinary events that are currently taking place there. At one time, the children of Italians born in America rarely asked their elders about news concerning the country that they had left many years previously. The aim of these questions was largely to verify the accuracy of some rumors disseminated by Americans regarding the poverty, crudeness of customs, and the low standard of living that were prevalent there. From that period in which one spoke of Italy only on occasions that related to the Royal House and to the Vatican or to opera performances by the tenor Enrico Caruso, the change in the attitude of the press and American public opinion regarding Italy and Italian has been remarkable. In order to confirm the little attention Italy had previously been granted in the press, the children of immigrants had formed an exaggerated idea of the baseness of its social and economic state to the point of considering it almost on par with any insignificant, little Balkan state. Fascism signaled Italy's hour in the spectrum of world politics. With growing amazement, the Italo-Americans saw the name of Italy appear more frequently in the newspapers. A day did not pass in which Mussolini and fascism were not in the headlines. No small number of Italo-Americans spontaneously admitted with ill-concealed astonishment: "We have never heard Italy mentioned so much since Mussolini gained power." However, there were other things that captured their attention: representatives from Italy on several occasions were received in Washington with uncommon distinction and officials of the great nations of Europe flocked to Rome seeking agreements, counsel, support, and directives. They take as an example what is being done in Italy, they mention the Italian institutions, and they discuss and use as comparison the Italian social measures. Consequently, this produces a great transformation in their minds. Italy was not the pitiful and backwards country in which nothing good could be found that they were led to believe. An enormous interest in the land of their fathers has been awakened in them: its history, its language, and its literature. This is seen in the continual increase of the number of students who enroll in Italian courses. Before, they were ashamed to speak in a language that revealed their origins: now, those who know some Italian take advantage of any opportunity to speak it and to master it. Others pull out their bits of dialect picked up in the home to show their Italian heritage and seriously regret not knowing more. And there is a growing number of middle school and university students who study Italian subjects: literary, historical, and artistic. Many have taken the route to Italy: they pursue their degree in Italian universities. It is true that there are many reasons for this: above all there is the limited space in the American universities, which is reserved for those students who have obtained a higher ranking. Nevertheless, if the regard for Italy was still what it once was, the students, who now go and ask for an advanced education in the land of their fathers, would have gone elsewhere. They would have gone to France, Belgium, Switzerland, Germany, and Austria. They have finally discovered the existence of a country that is also a part of them and where they will feel less foreign than in other places, a country where they have close relatives whom they had never seen and would have never seen: old grandparents at the bottom of a village in the Silla or the Abruzzo who will hug them crying with emotion; sisters and brothers of their mother and father who anxiously wait for them; and city-dwelling cousins who are anxious and curious to see the *American*, to hear him speak, observe how he acts and what impression Italy will have on him. Moreover, this old country that had been described to them as crumbling into the abyss of poverty and ignorance had institutes of high culture that could compete with the best in the world: they lacked perhaps the luxury, space, and abundance of archives, libraries and instructional material than those of the Americans, but in terms of seriousness of studies, intensity of research, and modernity of approaches they did not fear the comparison with any other nation. The spiritual and cultural atmosphere that was missing in America made them supremely interesting and gave a greater sense of seriousness and responsibility to those who complete their studies in countries with an old world culture that is not superimposed or extraneous to daily life but is an integral part of it. The difference is not missed by the parents who send their children to study in Italy but rather by those who keep them in America to take vocational courses. The latter often admit with a sigh of resignation mixed with a little envy: "I saw the children of a friend of mine who attended a university in Italy and returned for vacation. I don't know, but it seems they acquired a level of seriousness and maturity that those who study here do not have. They appear to be more well-rounded and more adult. My children and their fellow classmates at American universities always remain, in a certain sense, kids."

Without realizing it, they express a great truth. It's the impression shared by all those who have experience with both American and Italian students and who are in a position to make such comparisons.

The great respect and regard garnered by Italy in American public opinion is also found in the certain frequency of marriages between Italians and Americans, especially between American girls who go for some time to Italy to study or travel. At first, this occurred only among the higher social classes, in that international world of the aristocracy where the lines of ethnic and national distinction are almost unrecognizable. However, such unions have also recently spread among the high and lower middle class, which speaks more than any other factor in favor of the change in opinion regarding us and of the demise of a torrent of prejudices that caused American parents to faint upon hearing that one of their daughters had fallen in love with a *dago*. Shades of Teddy Roosevelt! These are precisely his words: "I always shivered at the thought that my daughter might one day marry a *dago*!"

Finally, there is a class of people whose heart jumps for joy in seeing this constant elevation of the Italian name in the favor and esteem of the entire world. It is a strange class of people whom a spiritualist would define as the reincarnation on American soil of human beings who were born, lived, and died in Italy and whose only passion was their own country. They are Italo-Americans who saw the light in America and have never visited the land of their fathers. Perhaps they do not expect to ever see it. But for Italy they have an enthusiastic and jealous passion that makes them seem almost abnormal, and they do not tolerate even the slightest criticism directed towards it. They have formed the idea of a perfect construction in both a material and moral sense, in its physical appearance and in the character of its inhabitants. How they arrived at such a conviction is a mystery. Often raised in poor families, no one spoke to them about Italy, no one presented them with an idea of the historical fascination that emanates from its stones, the inspiration of certain serene corners, its blazing skies, and the glow of its seashores. And yet, they see all these things, they see them as if they have had an otherworldly vision. They are capable of remaining enchanted for hours in front of certain paintings of courtyards, fountains, cobblestone roads of villages and country sides, quaint rustic homes protected by shady trees, and benches surrounded by ivy. It was the Italy that they had seen in their dreams and about which they daydreamed. The sensation is so great that they feel as if they have lived in those places in some previous life, have moved about those locations, were familiar with their hidden corners, are reminded of familiar scenes, and where they have rejoiced and loved. To complete the strangeness of their case, they speak Italian with such a fluency and self-confidence that they seem to have been born in Italy. They didn't go to school. No one taught them. However, the attention to their country of origin is so heartfelt and their adaptation and adjustment to an environment where they were born so painful that it makes one think of a sentence of perpetual exile with no hope. So powerful are their spiritual and ancestral imprints impressed in their character by a thousand-year-old race that they, born and raised in a foreign country, will feel perpetually alien there and will walk a *via crucis*, and will endure all the painful trials of the *sradicati* (*the uprooted*).

XI. IRREPARABLE DAMAGE

For a group of immigrants like ours who in their land of adoption had been totally overlooked, it is no small feat to have improved its status through a gradual change of public opinion, which is due as much to its intrinsic qualities as it is to Italy's being a country of first rank in the world. The Americans had tried to heap slurs and scorn on Italy in which it was depicted as belonging to a people who had fallen into the abyss of poverty and decay and as a nation of no importance on the world's stage that was incapable of governing itself and whose existence was only to be subservient to those who represented western civilization. For several centuries, Italy had fallen behind the pace of this civilization and it would never have been possible to get back in step with the most advanced nations. The children of our immigrants had ended up believing all the lies and scientific bunk, all the inconsistent assertions disseminated by deceptive and malicious propaganda. They were ashamed of their origins and did not have faith or respect for the country of their fathers. The political and social renewal of Italy inspired in them a new found pride. They no longer saw themselves as offshoots of an exotic and hybrid plant from which there is no hope to extract anything useful, a type of damaging weed transplanted in a foreign land. Fascism has given them a patent of nobility. In discussions and disputes with those of other nationalities, they often refer, and with obvious satisfaction, to their Roman origins, to the great periods of Italian civilization, and to the geniuses it produced. They give the impression of someone who, having been kept in conditions of inferiority as a result of his humble social state, has suddenly discovered the illustrious lineage to which he belongs. As we have seen, there has been a type of return to one's origins. Those who did not reapproach the original immigrant communities and did not feel the need to make direct contact with the land of their fathers for idealistic reasons did it for economic reasons. The crisis was the determining factor in this *falling back*, as the Americans say, on their original conditions. The Italo-Americans who detached themselves from their ethnic nucleus, swearing to never return and choosing instead to enter into an American environment and make a name for themselves, have always encountered enormous difficulties found in the impenetrable barrier of real prejudices, diffidence, jealousy, racial hatred, different upbringing, and strong incompatibilities of temperament. During the crisis, even the few accessible openings that allowed a slow stream of our people into the various categories of the American society were hermetically closed. This was more than anything else out of necessity. The scarce sources of income that were still active were carefully controlled so that they would not fall into the hands of intruders. The Americans became increasingly difficult with regard to those they considered foreigners even if they were born on American soil. Gone was the generosity, gone was the good nature, gone was the tolerance, and gone was the spirit of *good will* from which one took pleasure in seeing everyone making a living and doing well. They currently fight over every inch of land, arguing meticulously and bitterly over the intellectual and moral qualifications as well as the nationality of those who intend to invade a domain that they consider reserved for their activity. The Italo-Americans thus fell back into their Italian communities. They began to scrutinize, investigate, and analyze the economic possibilities of these groups that have been so disregarded to ensure whether they could make a living by settling among them and by benefitting from them as much as possible. All in all, this phenomenon can not be looked at with sympathy. These people, instead of forcing themselves to exercise their youthful energies in areas of activity not completely drained, remain in the Italo-American communities to compete with professionals, clerical workers, small merchants, and businessmen who came from Italy: a life that has become truly rough. The competition was so intense that it demoralized one's spirit, resulting in ferocious hostilities and even crimes.

For certain sectors, such as the professional one, things are getting worse each year. The plethora of professionals has become a scourge for the Italian community in America as it has always been in Italy, and particularly in the South. Coming rarely into contact with the basic productive operations of the American nation that would prove to be beneficial to their children, our fellow immigrants do not see any other future option but to choose the professional route. Just like in Italy, there are especially two areas that represent their concept of professions *par excellance*: doctor and lawyer. Still numerous, but to a lesser degree, are those graduates in engineering and pharmacy, professors of letters and modern languages. The bourgeoisie has maintained an almost religious respect for those areas of study that existed in Italy. They then inculcate this in their children, urging them or forcing them, when the opportunity arises, to embrace careers for which they are not cut out and will perpetually struggle in the mediocrity of their skills and in the difficulty of earning a living. The *cafoni* did the same thing. Following the example of the bourgeoisie, each time the financial conditions allowed them, they insisted on wanting their sons to become professionals. And even when their financial situation was far from flourishing, they were willing to make painful sacrifices to satisfy an entire life's ambition: to see their son become a professional. Such a gesture would be highly admirable in itself because this category demonstrates for the immigrants a desire to elevate themselves. Nonetheless, among the most vivid memories of their native town that has remained indelible in their mind was that of the doctor or lawyer as the pinnacle of the social hierarchy, along with the general respect that they enjoyed. How many times before setting out on the great journey did they imagine in their secret dreams of a miraculous change of position and of their son in the new land wearing a judicial gown or a white lab coat for the operating room! The destiny of their children had been sealed from that moment and the old humble farm laborers, drunken with joy, saw them emerge from the majestic universities with a degree under their arm. In a large number of cases, the new graduates, who would have preferred to follow other vocations, found nothing to do. Even when they have a wife and children, they remain for a long time dependent on their parents. They are victims mercilessly sacrificed to the fetish of the noble professions and high culture.

* * *

The recent return, for various reasons, of numerous children of immigrants to their original communities and their unexpected reawakening of interest in Italy and things Italian should not make us close our eyes to the tragic reality of all the past decades in which millions of our fellow countrymen and their children were definitively lost for Italy. They were the tragic years of abandonment and humiliation. No one cared for them and the fatherland was poor and decaying: the governments were content to rid themselves of them like a major inconvenience and to not hear anymore about them. The separation took place little by little: initially there was the death of those closest to them, then of other relatives and friends. The small properties that were still left in their native town were gradually sold and the entire family was beckoned to America. The immigrant was left without any connection that would keep him tied to his native land. He saw his children grow up around him, he requested American citizenship, and he changed his name. No need to hold this against him. That of a name, for example, whose change always results in being labeled a traitor, is in numerous cases a necessity. In Italy, it is not easy to explain this, especially to those who do not know the peculiarities of the English language. The Italian names are long and they contrast with the characteristic of English, which are monosyllabic. Besides, the sound never remains what it should be. When pronounced in English, Italian names sounded ridiculous and at times obscene. For numerous others, the difficulties of pronunciation were truly serious and the results were terribly mangled names. It was hilarious to see the surprise of certain parents who, after having sent their children to school for years, learn for the first time how their surnames are pronounced in the classes by teachers and other students. There are those who are even left dumbfounded and are unable to believe it. They never thought it would be possible. They were convinced that the name of the family was pronounced exactly as it was in Italy. In America, one of the first steps towards success of any kind is established by a short, easy on the ear name that is easy to pronounce. A long, complicated name that, as it happens to the foreign ones, is pronounced in a thousand different ways constitutes in itself a *handicap*, an obstacle to progress of any kind. Therefore, for the new generations, it was very difficult to resist the enormous pressures of their schoolteachers who were determined to Americanize the foreign names at all costs.

Consequently, numerous Italian names were lost to the point that it is not even possible to retrace their origins. An infinite number have been lost and keep disappearing with mixed marriages. How can one define any longer, even from the ethnic point of view, who is Italian and who is not Italian? Those youngsters with an Italian name are children of an Irish mother, and others of a Jewish mother. In some communities, particularly among the middle classes, there are many Italians who marry Irish girls. In large cities, a large number of Italian young men marry Jewish girls whom they see all day in the factories. The surprises of mixed marriages that America offers are many. Kids with an Italian surname have, among their ancestors, Scots, French, Spaniards with only a few diluted drops of Italian blood. You find yourself before some cases that leave you dumbfounded. A Nordic looking girl speaks perfect Italian and even the Neapolitan dialect. You ask her how long it has been since she came from Italy and she responds laughing that she was born in America of English parents and that, left an orphan, was adopted by an Italian or, to be more precise, Neapolitan family. A Sicilian girl (you learn this later) speaks to a group of people in a Slavic language. In a mining region where her parents brought her as a child, she grew up in the middle of families of Croatian miners. In an area of mountains and mines of the southern states, the present author bumped into a Calabrian family enlivened by the beauty of 22 children who were all healthy adults. The Italians at the location were limited to three or four families in all. These young men and women were married to people of all different nationalities. The mother, an attractive woman, who is still young and well-built, described the situation to me with a keen sense of humor: "Every now and then one of my children goes out and returns home with a wife or husband of another nationality. As if we were so few in our home! A few months ago one of my boys went to play a championship game of baseball in Texas and returned with an American wife. And this one here," she pointed to a youngster who hung around her legs, "is the child of one of my girls who married an Irish man. And that one there," as a young woman carrying a baby in her arms approached, "is the Scottish wife of another one of my boys. Another daughter of mine married a Greek. We've experienced all nationalities except for Hungarians!" she added as a way of concluding. To explain her last observation, one needs to know that there is a good number of Hungarian miners at that location.

Given the conditions in which we have attempted to offer some idea, it would not be easy to determine how many we could still call Italians. Perhaps they are around five million but increasingly diluted by a mixture of foreign blood. The case of those who would have liked to preserve themselves as Italians and were not able is painful. Distant and isolated in the middle of nowhere for reasons of employment, they had to yield to the hostile circumstances. Detached from the Italian communities and without schools that could teach them the language of their homeland, they are compelled, begrudgingly, to allow themselves to be assimilated. And it hurts when one finds small groups in remote places: they speak Italian haltingly, they tell you that they have been away from Italy for thirty or forty years, and they no longer hope to see it again. And their children? They only vaguely know that their parents were born some place in Europe. Not all could have been saved. However, if social services of former governments and organizations for national purposes had not been completely lacking, an enormous number of extremely precious elements would not have been lost at the expense of the ethnic potentiality and economic and productive capacity of our country.

XII. THE FUTURE OF ITALIANS IN AMERICA

As much as we have discussed Italian immigration to the United States, it cannot exactly be called a success. At least up to now. Nor could this have reasonably occured. Its principle mass was made up of the poorest, the most backwards, the most physically weak, and the least intellectually developed of our peninsula. There weighed on them age-old oppressions that had suffocated their creative instincts, destroyed their initiatives, and paralyzed any impulse to progress. They remained immobilized in a very long, dark night that, with brief intervals of splendor, had lasted 1500 years. It seemed that the light of dawn was not to be expected. Poverty, disease, superstition and ignorance had produced poor human types that were frail and scrawny in body, primitive in their ideas, and not well suited to the complexities of modern life. They could not bring to the new land a culture that they did not possess, nor could they circulate among the foreigners and transfer to their own children their homeland's language that they did not know. They were not capable of giving a significant contribution of original endeavors, technical or specialized expertise, bright imagination, fertile ideas and rediscovered inventiveness. Despite those very serious, early failures that hindered each step of the Italians as they set out to seek fortune, one cannot in good conscience claim that the tremendous effort, untiring work under hostile conditions and pathetic circumstances, cruel hardships, adversities and persecutions endured with an admirable strength of spirit have not created nothing and have ended up in complete failure. If one speaks of failure, it was the failure of the bourgeoisie. Besides having failed to serve as a guide and an example, the bourgeoisie only followed their own limited, selfish, personal end to squeeze from the productive mass of immigrants as much they could in order to return to Italy and be *galantuomini* with a financial base that was much more secure than when they left. The former peasants, laborers, and artisans who left their country never learned anything worthwhile from the representatives of the local bourgeoisie. On the contrary, from the examples provided by the bourgeoisie and on which they modeled themselves, they acquired a great number of defects: posturing, frivolousness, hardness, arrogance, and a tendency to quarrel. These traits make many of our fellow countrymen, who have lived for a long time in America and who have had the good fortune to have had notable financial success, at times feel ridiculous, other times intolerable, and sometimes both. The *nouveau riche* type has become everywhere the target of caricatures and biting satires: even in our communities the gentrified *cafone* is often detestable. However, the manners that have made him most repulsive are those that he has acquired from the bourgeoisie in his ardent ambition to imitate them, or those that the *galantuomini* were first able to instill and then make richly blossom in his mind as a means of benefitting their plans. The most common flattery used to lure the *cafone* and have him fall in a trap is that of playing to his vanity and giving him a sense of exaggerated social importance: praise in the newspaper for every action whether it be private or public, such as the appropriate announcements of family celebrations: baptisms, weddings, name days, and birthdays. And then there are the banquets given in his honor, on the occasion of departures and returns from some trip and those given for no apparent reason with the inevitable succession of speeches, toasts, adulation, and chants of praise so ridiculous and exaggerated that, if one wanted to believe them, one would think that the guest of honor is a great philanthropist or a world renowned thinker or inventor. But the ultimate seduction is that of some award, a cross of any kind that shines before his eyes like an illusion. The newly moneyed *cafone* cannot resist and always falls. At other times, groups develop that are real *rackets*, which draw him into the network and persuade him to untie his purse strings in compensation for meaningless entitlements from countries that are difficult to find on the map or that have completely disappeared as national entities. If he had not been so compromised by the intrigues of the bourgeoisie and demoralized by the systems with which the *galantuomini* have treated him, even the often belittled and hated figure of the newly moneyed *cafone* would have been of much greater benefit to the Italian communities. His money would not have gone to fuel fictitious and useless endeavors and to serve and satisfy ridiculous vanities but would have supported with greater effectiveness the initiatives aimed at the economic improvement and moral and intellectual advancement of the Italians of America.

* * *

Things being as they are, recriminations become useless. Our communities of America have inconsistencies and defects dating back to our origins that cannot be remedied. Therefore, it is out of the question to have any great illusions. And the most dangerous illusions are those of individuals who come to America unaware of the particular composition of our group of immigrants and who expect to deal with them as a uniform and compact mass that just left Italian shores. The type of Italian that they find beyond the Atlantic puzzles them and leaves them speechless, as if they were to find themselves for the first time in front of a new zoological species that no one had ever heard of. It's pointless to say that they run away crossing themselves.

What is needed is to study objectively what possibilities these new communities still offer from a national perspective and what is the best way for us not to miss the advantages and the capacity for development that this perspective offers. To pretend to preserve as Italian an entire mass of immigrants is an absurdity that only someone who has never been to America and has never seen an Italian community is naïve enough to imagine. And so, each year our communities become less Italian. The most damaging blow dealt to the *italianità* of our colonies, and what induced the separation from the country of origin, was the law that closed immigration almost completely and the subsequent measures that made the closure inevitable. The Americans knew what they were doing when they closed the dikes to the European flood. Then there are the mixed marriages and the gradual assimilation of the Italians into the American composite. The block slowly begins to crumble. The old immigrants die: with them goes a tradition, a period not only full of pain, of confusion, of misery but also quaint, colorful, and above all radiating hope and rendered romantic by a sense of adventure. It is unlikely that humanity will see a similar period. They are decades that defined an era: an era of exploration, of colonization, and of enhancement of the American continent. The old immigrants who see the world transformed before their eyes go back to that period with deep nostalgia and recall anecdotes, particular characteristics, and sad, happy, tragic, and ridiculous events: it was the time of their youth, of dreams, and of a faith in the future. One by one they disappear and take with them the memory of that era.

The children of immigrants, as we have seen, are an entirely different thing. They are able to salvage, maybe, about ten per cent of their forebears. What we mean by salvage is that this ten per cent will be able to form in America an *élite* that will perpetuate the memory of Italian migration and to whom will be entrusted the patrimony of the language and of the Italian culture that they will preserve and spread on foreign soil. With the formation of such an *élite*, one must try to save what is still salvageable of the Italian ethnic stock. It would be an error to insist on returning to the fold those who have already abandoned it for quite some time with such a dispersion of energy that does not lead to any conclusion. All the forces must be concentrated on those initiatives and those institutions that are dedicated to the formation of an Italian *élite* who are aware that great benefits will come from the land of origin and to the country where it had its beginnings. These chosen ranks will assume the task of dispelling misunderstandings, promote consensus between the two nations, foster more understanding towards one another, and interpret each other's ideals and aspirations. Such an aristocracy of intelligence and spirit could fulfill the lofty mission of intensifying the cultural exchanges between Italy and the United States and with them a mutual knowledge and sympathy. The elimination of prejudices and diffidence of a lifetime should be entrusted to this. The economy of the two countries would benefit from the mutual integration of the production and reactivation of trade. The members of this *élite* should be that connection, interpreters in a spiritual sense, messengers of good will, noble promoters of exchanges of what is best in the two countries. No time is better than right now. Never before has there been such an interest in the immigrants' descendants in Italy, its government, its institutions, its language, and its culture. One needs to take advantage of this opportunity and move towards these children of our people and satisfy the noble thirst for knowledge and also for the affection that brings it to life. It would be a crime to force them to fall back hopelessly into the cold world of American hybridity. However, even here it is necessary to proceed with caution and not commit errors at the cost of losing them forever. Best not to raise suspicion and mistrust by pretending that they are or will become what they are not. In other words, that they stop being Americans. This mindless claim, maintained by those who have no practical experience with America and its communities and whose sole aim is to draw attention to their misplaced and misguided zeal, has caused the definitive alienation and hostility for everything that is Italian to a large number of sensible, intelligent youths who, approached differently, would become better promoters of Italian spirit and thought. And here we cannot help but celebrate the initiatives advocated by the Duce as the most effective in instilling a love for our country in the minds of the children of Italians abroad and in promoting an interest and knowledge of the homeland. We are referring to the summer camps for the small children of expatriates and the granting of free trips to students of Italian origin who have succeeded in school. You should have seen the eagerness of these students as they waited for the moment of departure and the enthusiasm with which they ask about news of Italy, consult their maps, and push themselves to improve their knowledge of the language! They will be the best ambassadors of *italianità* among their fellow companions of Italian origin as well as their American companions. They will form tomorrow's *élite* who, we hope, will emerge to perpetuate the Italian civilization in the New Continent.

NOTE

This book was written and submitted to the publisher when the Italo-Abyssian conflict broke out. In a chapter of the present volume, we elaborated on the change in sentiments of the Italo-American youth regarding the land from where their fathers came. However, what occurred during the war that has recently come to an end is incredible. The timid and uncertain impulses that tend to restore confidence in a centuries-old culture and to re-unite spiritually with the country where the race to which they belong has its origins has assumed the appearance of an overwhelming movement. The Italo-American youths were the most tenacious against those who wanted to cross our path. They were the ones who were really furious against the world power that, while being satiated with territories, dominance, and wealth, was obstinate in not recognizing the need for the development of a people on the rise. Italy appeared to them under a new light. It began with the youths in the elementary schools who countered with words and fists every offense against the Italian name, every hostile and scornful comment from their companions of other ethnic groups. And it was moving to see with what fervor these little Italian offspring, who were born in America, ask their parents news about the war, the Italian army, and all of Italy. In schools, factories, and public places, the Italo-Americans were the most passionate and relentless in discussions: they fought, they argued, they defended Italian causes against hostile groups. Many who were born in America sought to enroll in the Italian army, go to Africa and contribute to the building of the Italian empire.

The behavior of our communities on American soil was simply remarkable. Affected as they are by the nearly six year crisis, they found a way to send to the homeland approximately 20 million lire. Poor women relinquished antique necklaces, old bracelets, earrings, rings, and dear memories of all kinds in order to convert them into money to be sent to Italy. Nearly 50,000 iron rings were distributed among the Italian communities in America, corresponding to as many gold rings dedicated to the homeland.

But what truly arouses a sense of boundless admiration and is cause for reflection is to see that that amount of money mentioned above consists in large part of small offerings of a dollar, two dollars, and even a half dollar, that the poor families and isolated workers, who are barely able to grab on the fly a day or two of work, took bread from their mouths in order to send money to their country of origin that was intent on overcoming a crisis out of which a greater, more powerful, and more respected Italy will have emerged.

The wealthy and the privileged corresponded to barely 10 per cent of the number of immigrants. The thesis that has been treated extensively in this book is reaffirmed here. It is the *cafone* who still represents the foundation of every movement of *italianità* on American soil, a serious *italianità* that expresses itself with facts and not with bombastic speeches and a deluge of rhetorical phrases. It is the *cafone* who represents the heart and economic force of any action that needs to be conducted among the Italian communities of America. The rest is nothing but parasitism, pompous vanity, a tendency to exaggerate and to show off, all things that lead to disorder, division, and bias, producing profound disappointments that, in a foreign country, do more harm to the cause of *italianità* than a lost war.

ABOUT THE AUTHOR

AMERIGO RUGGIERO was born on July 31, 1878 in the southern Italian town of Grottole, located in the province of Matera. At an early age, he moved with his family to the nearby town of Grassano. He received degrees in Medicine and Surgery and in Veterinary Science at the University of Naples Federico II. During his student years in Naples, he became an activist in the Italian Socialist Party. His political militancy led to his arrest in Rome and imprisonment in Naples. In 1907, he immigrated to New York, where he joined his brother, a licensed pharmacist, and where he collaborated with various newspapers and magazines. Following the outbreak of World War I, he first-sided with the anti-interventionists but then decided to return to Italy and participate as a volunteer in the Alpini corps as a veterinary lieutenant. After practicing medicine for two years near Rome, he returned to the United States in 1922 to focus on journalism. He served as a foreign correspondent in the United States for the Turin newspaper *La Stampa* from 1929 into the 1940s, writing on such topics as economics, sports, American politics and society, and the conditions of the Italian immigrants. It was in this latter role that he gained fame as Italy's leading correspondent from New York. Ruggiero also contributed to other major Italian newspapers, including *Il Mattino* of Naples, *Il Messaggero* of Rome, *La Nazione* of Florence, and the *Gazzetta del Popolo* of Turin, and to numerous Italian American newspapers and magazines. He served as managing editor of the Italian American weekly *La Settimana*, published in New York between 1935 and 1937 and, during the 1950s, he was a special foreign correspondent to *Divagando*, the most widely read Italian American magazine in the United States. In addition to the volume *Italiani in America*, Ruggiero published *L'America al bivio* (1934) with Giulio Einaudi Editore, whose cover was designed by Carlo Levi. Ruggiero died in Grassano on December 4, 1959.

ABOUT THE EDITOR AND TRANSLATOR

MARK PIETRALUNGA is the Victor R. B. Oelschläger Professor in the Department of Modern Languages and Linguistics at Florida State University, where he teaches courses in Italian Studies and where he served as Chair for sixteen years. He earned his degrees from UCLA (BA in English) and UC Berkeley (MA and PhD in Italian). He was Book Review Editor for the journal *Italica* for many years and now serves as one of its Associate Editors. He is also Associate Editor for the journal of the Italian American Studies Association. He is the author, editor, and translator of numerous books and articles on 20th century Italian literature and culture, translation studies, post war Italian narrative, and Italian American studies. His books include *Beppe Fenoglio and English Literature: The Study of the Writer as Translator* (1987; also in Italian), P.B. Shelley's *Prometeo slegato*, translated by Cesare Pavese (1997), *Quaderno di Traduzioni* di Beppe Fenoglio (2000), *Cesare Pavese & Anthony Chiuminatto: Their Correspondence* (2007), and *Cesare Pavese's Long Journey: A Critical Analytical Study* by Giose Rimanelli (2019). In 2019, he was the recipient of the American Association Teachers of Italian (AATI) Distinguished Service Award in recognition of his achievements in teaching and research, together with a strong commitment to service, in the fields of Italian language, literature, and civilization.

CROSSINGS
AN INTERSECTION OF CULTURES

Crossings is dedicated to the publication of Italian-language literature and translations from Italian to English.

Rodolfo Di Biasio. *Wayfarers Four*. Translated by Justin Vitello. 1998. ISBN 1-88419-17-9. Vol 1.

Isabella Morra. *Canzoniere: A Bilingual Edition*. Translated by Irene Musillo Mitchell. 1998. ISBN 1-88419-18-6. Vol 2.

Nevio Spadone. *Lus*. Translated by Teresa Picarazzi. 1999. ISBN 1-88419-22-4. Vol 3.

Flavia Pankiewicz. *American Eclipses*. Translated by Peter Carravetta. Introduction by Joseph Tusiani. 1999. ISBN 1-88419-23-2. Vol 4.

Dacia Maraini. *Stowaway on Board*. Translated by Giovanna Bellesia and Victoria Offredi Poletto. 2000. ISBN 1-88419-24-0. Vol 5.

Walter Valeri, editor. *Franca Rame: Woman on Stage*. 2000. ISBN 1-88419-25-9. Vol 6.

Carmine Biagio Iannace. *The Discovery of America*. Translated by William Boelhower. 2000. ISBN 1-88419-26-7. Vol 7.

Romeo Musa da Calice. *Luna sul salice*. Translated by Adelia V. Williams. 2000. ISBN 1-88419-39-9. Vol 8.

Marco Paolini & Gabriele Vacis. *The Story of Vajont*. Translated by Thomas Simpson. 2000. ISBN 1-88419-41-0. Vol 9.

Silvio Ramat. *Sharing A Trip: Selected Poems*. Translated by Emanuel di Pasquale. 2001. ISBN 1-88419-43-7. Vol 10.

Raffaello Baldini. *Page Proof*. Edited by Daniele Benati. Translated by Adria Bernardi. 2001. ISBN 1-88419-47-X. Vol 11.

Maura Del Serra. *Infinite Present*. Translated by Emanuel di Pasquale and Michael Palma. 2002. ISBN 1-88419-52-6. Vol 12.

Dino Campana. *Canti Orfici*. Translated and Notes by Luigi Bonaffini. 2003. ISBN 1-88419-56-9. Vol 13.

Roberto Bertoldo. *The Calvary of the Cranes*. Translated by Emanuel di Pasquale. 2003. ISBN 1-88419-59-3. Vol 14.

Paolo Ruffilli. *Like It or Not*. Translated by Ruth Feldman and James Laughlin. 2007. ISBN 1-88419-75-5. Vol 15.

Giuseppe Bonaviri. *Saracen Tales*. Translated Barbara De Marco. 2006. ISBN 1-88419-76-3. Vol 16.

Leonilde Frieri Ruberto. *Such Is Life*. Translated Laura Ruberto. Introduction by Ilaria Serra. 2010. ISBN 978-1-59954-004-7. Vol 17.

Gina Lagorio. *Tosca the Cat Lady*. Translated by Martha King. 2009. ISBN 978-1-59954-002-3. Vol 18.

Marco Martinelli. *Rumore di acque*. Translated and edited by Thomas Simpson. 2014. ISBN 978-1-59954-066-5. Vol 19.

Emanuele Pettener. *A Season in Florida*. Translated by Thomas De Angelis. 2014. ISBN 978-1-59954-052-2. Vol 20.

Angelo Spina. *Il cucchiaio trafugato*. 2017. ISBN 978-1-59954-112-9. Vol 21.

Michela Zanarella. *Meditations in the Feminine*. Translated by Leanne Hoppe. 2017. ISBN 978-1-59954-110-5. Vol 22.

Francesco "Kento" Carlo. *Resistenza Rap*. Translated by Emma Gainsforth and Siân Gibby. 2017. ISBN 978-1-59954-112-9. Volume 23.

Kossi Komla-Ebri. *EMBAR-RACE-MENTS*. Translated by Marie Orton. 2019. ISBN 978-1-59954-124-2. Volume 24.

Angelo Spina. *Immagina la prossima mossa*. 2019. ISBN 978-1-59954-153-2. Volume 25.

Luigi Lo Cascio. *Othello*. Translated by Gloria Pastorino. 2020. ISBN 978-1-59954-158-7. Vol 26.

Sante Candeloro. *Puzzle*. Translated by Fred L. Gardaphe. 2020. ISBN 978-1-59954-165-5. Vol 27.

CPSIA information can be obtained
at www.ICGtesting.com
Printed in the USA
BVHW081110180920
588316BV00002B/152